180 Days of PROBLEM SOLVING
for Kindergarten

- ? Think
- Plan
- Solve
- Explain

2+2=4

Author
Jessica Hathaway, M.S.Ed.

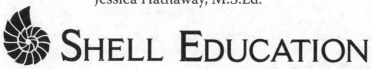

SHELL EDUCATION

For information on how this resource meets national and other state standards, see pages 4–7. You may also review this information by visiting our website at www.teachercreatedmaterials.com/administrators/correlations/ and following the on-screen directions.

Publishing Credits

Corinne Burton, M.A.Ed., *Publisher*; Conni Medina, M.A.Ed., *Managing Editor*; Emily R. Smith, M.A.Ed., *Series Developer*; Diana Kenney, M.A.Ed., NBCT, *Content Director*; Paula Makridis, M.A.Ed., *Editor*; Stacy Monsman, M.A.Ed., *Editor*; Lee Aucoin, *Multimedia Designer*; Kyleena Harper, *Assistant Editor*; Kevin Pham, *Graphic Designer*

Image Credits

All images from iStock and Shutterstock.

Standards

© 2010 Copyright. National Governors Association Center for Best Practices and Council of Chief State School Officers. All rights reserved. (CCSS)

Shell Education

A division of Teacher Created Materials
5301 Oceanus Drive
Huntington Beach, CA 92649-1030

www.tcmpub.com/shell-education
ISBN 978-1-4258-1612-4
©2017 Shell Education Publishing, Inc.

Printed in USA. WOR004

TABLE OF CONTENTS

INTRODUCTION

The Need for Practice

To be successful in today's mathematics classrooms, students must deeply understand both concepts and procedures so that they can discuss and demonstrate their understanding during the problem-solving process. Demonstrating understanding is a process that must be continually practiced for students to be successful. Practice is especially important to help students apply their concrete, conceptual understanding during each step of the problem-solving process.

Understanding Assessment

In addition to providing opportunities for frequent practice, teachers must be able to assess students' problem-solving skills. This is important so that teachers can adequately address students' misconceptions, build on their current understandings, and challenge them appropriately. Assessment is a long-term process that involves careful analysis of student responses from discussions, projects, practice pages, or tests. When analyzing the data, it is important for teachers to reflect on how their teaching practices may have influenced students' responses and to identify those areas where additional instruction may be required. In short, the data gathered from assessments should be used to inform instruction: slow down, speed up, or reteach. This type of assessment is called *formative assessment*.

HOW TO USE THIS BOOK

180 Days of Problem Solving offers teachers and parents problem-solving activities for each day of the school year. Students will build their problem-solving skills as they develop a deeper understanding of mathematical concepts and apply these concepts to real-life situations. This series will also help students improve their critical-thinking and reasoning skills, use visual models when solving problems, approach problems in multiple ways, and solve multi-step non-routine word problems.

Easy-to-Use and Standards-Based

These daily activities reinforce grade-level skills across a variety of mathematical concepts. Each day provides a full practice page, making the activities easy to prepare and implement as part of a classroom routine, at the beginning of each mathematics lesson as a warm-up or Problem of the Day, or as homework. Students can work on the practice pages independently or in cooperative groups. The practice pages can also be utilized as diagnostic tools, formative assessments, or summative assessments, which can direct differentiated small-group instruction during Mathematics Workshop.

Domains and Practice Standards

The chart below indicates the mathematics domains addressed and practice standards applied throughout this book. The subsequent chart shows the breakdown of which mathematics standard is covered in each week.

Note: Students may not have deep understanding of some topics of this book. Remember to assess students based on their problem-solving skills and not exclusively on their content knowledge.

Grade-Level Domains	Practice Standards
1. Counting and Cardinality	1. Make sense of problems and persevere in solving them.
2. Operations and Algebraic Thinking	2. Reason abstractly and quantitatively.
3. Number and Operations in Base Ten	3. Construct viable arguments and critique the reasoning of others.
4. Measurement and Data	4. Model with mathematics.
5. Geometry	5. Use appropriate tools strategically.
	6. Attend to precision.
	7. Look for and make use of structure.
	8. Look for and express regularity in repeated reasoning.

HOW TO USE THIS BOOK (cont.)

College-and-Career Readiness Standards

Below is a list of mathematical standards that are addressed throughout this book. Each week students solve problems related to the same mathematical topic.

Week	Standard
1	Count to 5 by ones.
2	Count to 10 by ones.
3	Count to answer "how many?" questions about as many as 10 things arranged in a line, a rectangular array, or a circle, or in a scattered configuration; given a number from 1–10, count out that many objects.
4	Count forward beginning from a given number within the known sequence (instead of having to begin at 1).
5	Understand the relationship between numbers and quantities; connect counting to cardinality. Understand that each successive number name refers to a quantity that is one larger.
6	Write numbers from 0 to 5. Represent a number of objects with a written numeral 0–5 (with 0 representing a count of no objects). Understand the relationship between numbers and quantities; connect counting to cardinality.
7	Write numbers from 6 to 10. Represent a number of objects with a written numeral 6–10. Understand the relationship between numbers and quantities; connect counting to cardinality.
8	Write numbers from 11 to 20. Represent a number of objects with a written numeral 11–20. Understand the relationship between numbers and quantities; connect counting to cardinality.
9	Count to 100 by tens.
10	Identify whether the number of objects in one group is equal to the number of objects in another group, e.g., by using matching and counting strategies.
11	Identify whether the number of objects in one group is greater than the number of objects in another group, e.g., by using matching and counting strategies.
12	Identify whether the number of objects in one group is less than the number of objects in another group, e.g., by using matching and counting strategies.
13	Compare two numbers between 1 and 5 presented as written numerals.

14	Compare two numbers between 1 and 10 presented as written numerals.
15	Classify objects by size; count the numbers of objects in each category and sort the categories by count.
16	Classify objects by color; count the numbers of objects in each category and sort the categories by count.
17	Classify objects into given categories; count the numbers of objects in each category and sort the categories by count.
18	Describe measurable attributes of objects, such as length or weight. Describe several measurable attributes of a single object.
19	Directly compare two objects with a measurable attribute in common, to see which object has "more of"/"less of" the attribute, and describe the difference.
20	Represent addition with objects, fingers, mental images, drawings, sounds (e.g., claps), acting out situations, verbal explanations, expressions, or equations. Fluently add within 5.
21	Represent addition with objects, fingers, mental images, drawings, sounds (e.g., claps), acting out situations, verbal explanations, expressions, or equations. Add within 10.
22	Solve addition word problems, and add and within 10, e.g., by using objects or drawings to represent the problem
23	Decompose numbers less than or equal to 10 into pairs in more than one way, e.g., by using objects or drawings, and record each decomposition by a drawing or equation (e.g., 5 = 2 + 3 and 5 = 4 + 1).
24	For any number from 1 to 9, find the number that makes 10 when added to the given number, e.g., by using objects or drawings, and record the answer with a drawing or equation.
25	Represent subtraction with objects, fingers, mental images, drawings, sounds (e.g., claps), acting out situations, verbal explanations, expressions, or equations. Fluently subtract within 5.
26	Represent subtraction with objects, fingers, mental images, drawings, sounds (e.g., claps), acting out situations, verbal explanations, expressions, or equations. Subtract within 10.
27	Represent subtraction with objects, fingers, mental images, drawings, sounds (e.g., claps), acting out situations, verbal explanations, expressions, or equations. Solve subtraction word problems, and subtract within 10.
28	Compose numbers from 11 to 19 into ten ones and some further ones, e.g., by using objects or drawings, and record each composition by a drawing or equation (such as 18 = 10 + 8); understand that these numbers are composed of ten ones and one, two, three, four, five, six, seven, eight, or nine ones.

29	Decompose numbers from 11 to 19 into ten ones and some further ones, e.g., by using objects or drawings, and record each decomposition by a drawing or equation (such as 18 = 10 + 8); understand that these numbers are composed of ten ones and one, two, three, four, five, six, seven, eight, or nine ones.
30	Correctly name two-dimensional shapes regardless of their orientations or overall size.
31	Analyze and compare two-dimensional shapes, in different sizes and orientations, using informal language to describe their similarities, differences, parts (e.g., number of sides and vertices/"corners") and other attributes (e.g., having sides of equal length).
32	Compose simple shapes to form larger shapes.
33	Describe objects in the environment using names of shapes, and describe the relative positions of these objects using terms such as above, below, beside, in front of, behind, and next to. Model shapes in the world by building shapes from components (e.g., sticks and clay balls) and drawing shapes.
34	Correctly name three-dimensional shapes regardless of their orientations or overall size.
35	Analyze and compare three-dimensional shapes, in different sizes and orientations, using informal language to describe their similarities, differences, parts (e.g., number of sides and vertices/"corners") and other attributes (e.g., having sides of equal length).
36	Identify shapes as two-dimensional (lying in a plane, "flat") or three-dimensional ("solid"). Analyze and compare two- and three-dimensional shapes, in different sizes and orientations, using informal language to describe their similarities, differences, parts (e.g., number of sides and vertices/"corners") and other attributes (e.g., having sides of equal length).

HOW TO USE THIS BOOK (cont.)

Using the Practice Pages

The activity pages provide practice and assessment opportunities for each day of the school year. Students focus on one grade-level skill each week. The five-day plan requires students to think about the problem-solving process, use visual models, draw a picture or model, and solve multi-step, non-routine word problems. For this grade level, teachers may complete the pages together as a class, or students may work in cooperative groups. Teachers may prepare packets of weekly practice pages for the classroom or for homework.

 Day 1–Think About It!
For the first day of each week, the focus is on thinking about the problem-solving process. Students might draw pictures or answer questions about a problem. The goal is to understand the process of solving a problem more so than finding the solution.

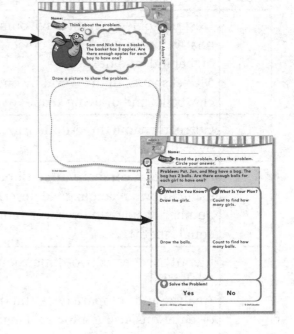

 Day 2–Solve It!
On the second day of each week, students solve a routine problem based on the thinking process from Day 1. Students think about the information given in the problem, decide on a plan, and solve the problem. Ask students to verbally explain their solutions and strategies.

 Day 3–Picture It!
On day three, a visual representation (e.g., picture or model) is shown as a strategy for solving a problem. Students use this visual model to solve a similar problem.

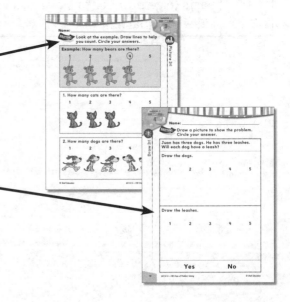

 Day 4–Draw It!
On the fourth day, students solve a problem by drawing a picture or using a visual model. Students may use the same strategy as shown in Day 3 or may choose their own strategy.

#51612—180 Days of Problem Solving   © Shell Education

HOW TO USE THIS BOOK (cont.)

Day 5–Challenge Yourself!
On day five, students are presented with a multi-step, non-routine problem. Students analyze a problem, think about different strategies, develop a plan, and solve the problem.

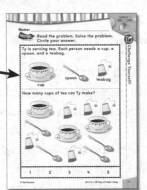

Using the Resources

The following resources will be helpful to students as they complete the activity pages. Print copies of these resources and provide them to students to keep at their desks. These resources are available as Adobe(R) PDFs online. A complete list of the available documents is provided on page 211. To access the digital resources, go to this website: http://www.tcmpub.com/downlead-files. Enter this code: 56796259. Follow the on-screen directions.

Practice Page Rubric can be found on page 203 and in the Digital Resources (rubric.pdf). The rubric can be used to assess students' mathematical understanding of the weekly concept and steps in the problem-solving process. The rubric should be shared with students so they know what is expected of them.

Problem-Solving Framework can be found on page 209 and in the Digital Resources (framework.pdf). Students can reference each step of the problem-solving process as they complete the practice pages during the week.

Problem-Solving Strategies can be found on page 210 and in the Digital Resources (strategies.pdf). Students may want to reference this page when choosing strategies as they solve problems throughout the week.

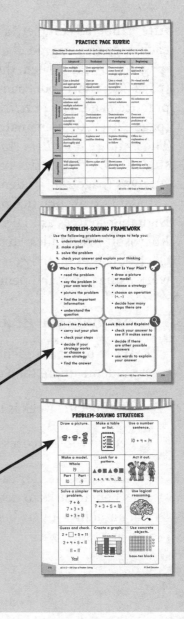

HOW TO USE THIS BOOK (cont.)

Diagnostic Assessment

Teachers can use the practice pages as diagnostic assessments. The data analysis tools included with the book enable teachers or parents to quickly score students' work and monitor their progress. Teachers and parents can quickly see which steps in the problem-solving process students need to target further to develop proficiency.

After students complete a week of practice pages, each page can be graded using the answer key (pages 193–202). Then, the *Practice Page Rubric* (page 203; rubric.pdf) can be used to score each practice page. The *Practice Page Item Analysis* (pages 204–207; itemanalysis.pdf) can be completed. The *Practice Page Item Analysis* can be used to record students' Day 5 practice page score, while the *Student Item Analysis* (page 208; studentitem.pdf) can be used to record a student's daily practice page score. These charts are also provided in the Digital Resources as PDFs, Microsoft Word® files (itemanalysis.docx; studentitem.docx), and Microsoft Excel® files (itemanalysis.xlsx; studentitem.xlsx). Teachers can input data into the electronic files directly on the computer, or they can print the pages and analyze students' work using paper and pencil.

To Complete the Practice Page Item Analysis

- Write or type students' names in the far-left column. Depending on the number of students, more than one copy of the form may be needed or you may need to add rows.

- The specific week is indicated across the tops of the charts.

- Record rubric scores for the Day 5 practice page in the appropriate column.

- Add the scores for each student. Place that sum in the far-right column. Use these scores as benchmarks to determine how each student is performing after a six-week period. This allows for six benchmarks during the year that can be used to gather formative diagnostic data.

HOW TO USE THIS BOOK *(cont.)*

To Complete the Student Item Analysis

- Write or type the student's name in the top row. This form tracks the ongoing process of each student, so one copy per student is necessary.

- The specific day is indicated across the top of each chart.

- Record the student's rubric score for each practice page in the appropriate column.

- Add the scores for the student. Place that sum in the far-right column. Use these scores as benchmarks to determine how the student is performing each week. These benchmarks can be used to gather formative diagnostic data.

Using the Results to Differentiate Instruction

Once results are gathered and analyzed, teachers can use the results to inform the way they differentiate instruction. The data can help determine which mathematical concepts and steps in the problem-solving process are the most difficult for students and which students need additional instructional support and continued practice.

Whole-Class Support

The results of the diagnostic analysis may show that the entire class is struggling with a particular mathematical concept or problem-solving step. If these concepts or problem-solving steps have been taught in the past, this indicates that further instruction or reteaching is necessary. If these concepts or steps have not been taught in the past, this data is a great preassessment and may demonstrate that students do not have a working knowledge of the concepts or steps. Thus, careful planning for the length of the unit(s) or lesson(s) must be considered, and additional front-loading may be required.

Small-Group or Individual Support

The results of the diagnostic analysis may show that an individual student or small group of students is struggling with a particular mathematical concept or problem-solving step. If these concepts or steps have been taught in the past, this indicates that further instruction or reteaching is necessary. These students can be pulled to a small group for further instruction on the concept(s) or step(s), while other students work independently. Students may also benefit from extra practice using games or computer-based resources. Teachers can also use the results to help identify individual students or groups of proficient students who are ready for enrichment or above-grade-level instruction. These groups may benefit from independent learning contracts or more challenging activities.

Digital Resources

The Digital Resources contain diagnostic pages and additional resources, such as the *Problem-Solving Framework* and *Problem-Solving Strategies* pages, for students. The list of resources in the Digital Resources can be found on page 211.

STANDARDS CORRELATIONS

Shell Education is committed to producing educational materials that are research and standards based. In this effort, we have correlated all of our products to the academic standards of all 50 states, the District of Columbia, the Department of Defense Dependents Schools, and all Canadian provinces.

How to Find Standards Correlations

To print a customized correlation report of this product for your state, visit our website at http://www.tcmpub.com/shell-education. If you require assistance in printing correlation reports, please contact our Customer Service Department at 1-877-777-3450.

Purpose and Intent of Standards

The Every Student Succeeds Act (ESSA) mandates that all states adopt challenging academic standards that help students meet the goal of college and career readiness. While many states already adopted academic standards prior to ESSA, the act continues to hold states accountable for detailed and comprehensive standards.

Standards are designed to focus instruction and guide adoption of curricula. Standards are statements that describe the criteria necessary for students to meet specific academic goals. They define the knowledge, skills, and content students should acquire at each level. Standards are also used to develop standardized tests to evaluate students' academic progress.

Teachers are required to demonstrate how their lessons meet state standards. State standards are used in the development of all of our products, so educators can be assured they meet the academic requirements of each state.

The activities in this book are aligned to today's national and state-specific college-and-career readiness standards. The chart on page 4 lists the domains and practice standards addressed throughout this book. A more detailed chart on pages 5–7 correlates the specific mathematics content standards to each week.

Name: _____

  Think about the problem.

Sam and Nick have a basket. The basket has 3 apples. Are there enough apples for each boy to have one?

Draw a picture to show the problem.

Solve It!

Name: _____

DIRECTIONS: Read the problem. Solve the problem. Circle your answer.

Problem: Pat, Jan, and Meg have a bag. The bag has 2 balls. Are there enough balls for each girl to have one?

? What Do You Know?

Draw the girls.

Draw the balls.

What Is Your Plan?

Count to find how many girls.

Count to find how many balls.

 Solve the Problem!

Yes   **No**

Picture It!

Name: _____

 **DIRECTIONS:** Look at the example. Draw lines to help you count. Circle your answers.

Example: How many bears are there?

1   2   3   ④   5

1. How many cats are there?

1   2   3   4   5

2. How many dogs are there?

1   2   3   4   5

#51612—180 Days of Problem Solving

Name: _____

Draw It!

DIRECTIONS: Draw a picture to show the problem. Circle your answer.

Juan has three dogs. He has three leashes. Will each dog have a leash?

Draw the dogs.

1   2   3   4   5

Draw the leashes.

1   2   3   4   5

Yes   No

Name: _____

DIRECTIONS:
Read the problem. Solve the problem.
Circle your answer.

Challenge Yourself!

Ty is serving tea. Each person needs a cup, a spoon, and a teabag.

cup

spoon

teabag

How many cups of tea can Ty make?

1   2   3   4   5

Think About It!

Name: _____

DIRECTIONS: Think about the problem.

There are seven bears.
Each bear wears a hat.
How many hats are there?

Draw a picture to show the problem.

Name: _____

 **DIRECTIONS:** Read the problem. Solve the problem. Circle your answer.

Solve It!

Problem: There are nine flowers. Each flower has one leaf. How many leaves are there?

 What Do You Know?

Circle the number of flowers.

1 2 3 4 5

6 7 8 9 10

What Is Your Plan?

Draw the leaves.

 Solve the Problem!

1 2 3 4 5 6 7 8 9 10

Picture It!

Name: _____

DIRECTIONS: Look at the example. Draw lines to solve the problem. Circle your answer.

Example: Each pen has a cap. How many caps are there?

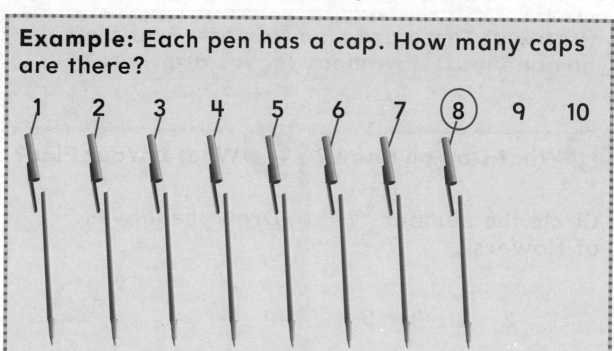

1   2   3   4   5   6   7   ⑧   9   10

Each cup has a straw. How many straws are there?

1   2   3   4   5   6   7   8   9   10

#51612—180 Days of Problem Solving

© Shell Education

Name: _____

DIRECTIONS: Draw a picture to show the problem. Circle your answer.

There are 8 boys. Each boy has a baseball. How many baseballs are there?

1   2   3   4   5   6   7   8   9   10

Draw It!

Challenge Yourself!

Name: _____

DIRECTIONS: Read the problem. Solve the problem. Circle the answer.

Ann wants to mail 6 birthday cards. Each card needs an envelope and a stamp.

card

envelope

stamp

Can Ann mail 6 birthday cards?

           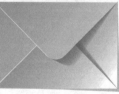  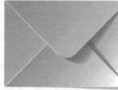

Yes   No

Name: _____

DIRECTIONS: Think about the problem.

Does each group have the same number of stars?

Which group looks like it has more stars?

Group 1

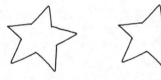

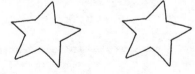
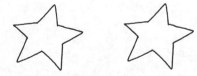

Group 2

Solve It!

Name: _____

Read the problem. Solve the problem. Circle your answers.

Problem: How many suns are in each box?

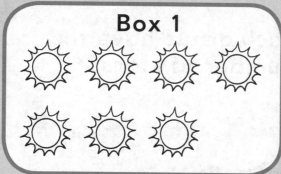

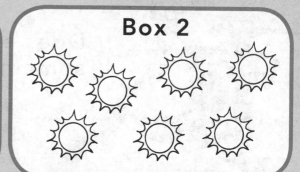

? What Do You Know?

_____

Each box has ___ suns ___.

🔑 What Is Your Plan?

Count the suns in each box.

💡 Solve the Problem!

Box 1: 1   2   3   4   5   6   7   8   9   10

Box 2: 1   2   3   4   5   6   7   8   9   10

#51612—180 Days of Problem Solving

Name: _____

 DIRECTIONS: Look at the example. Count to solve the problems. Circle your answers.

Picture It!

Example: How many toy cars does each kid have?

Joe's cars

1   2   3   4   5   6   (7)   8   9   10

Amy's cars

1   2   3   4   5   6   7   8   (9)   10

How many toy rings does each kid have?

Sally's rings

1   2   3   4   5   6   7   8   9   10

Rosa's rings

1   2   3   4   5   6   7   8   9   10

Draw It!

Name: _____

Draw a picture to show the problem. Circle your answers.

Draw five happy faces in Box 2. Do the boxes have the same number of happy faces?

Box 1

| 1 | 2 | 3 | 4 | 5 | 6 | 7 | 8 | 9 | 10 |

Box 2

| 1 | 2 | 3 | 4 | 5 | 6 | 7 | 8 | 9 | 10 |

Yes   **No**

Name: _____

 DIRECTIONS: Read the problem. Solve the problem. Circle your answer.

How old are you? Draw dots to show the number in Box 2. Compare the boxes.

Box 1	Box 2

Do the boxes have the same number of dots?

Yes   No

Think About It!

Name: _____

DIRECTIONS:
Think about the problem.

Cindy counts her coins. She counts on from 3. How many coins are there in all?

What are the ways you could count the coins?

3

Name: _____

 **DIRECTIONS:** Read the problem. Solve the problem. Circle your answers.

Problem: Count the marbles. Start at 2. How many marbles are there in all?

? What Do You Know?

How many marbles are in the circle?

1   2   3   4   5

6   7   8   9   10

🔑 What Is Your Plan?

Show how to count the marbles.

1   2

💡 Solve the Problem!

1   2   3   4   5   6   7   8   9   10

Picture It!

Name: _____

DIRECTIONS: Look at the example. Solve the problem. Circle your answer.

Example: Count the berries. Start at 5. How many berries are there in all?

1   2   3   4   5   6   7   (8)   9   10

Count the crayons. Start at 3. How many crayons are there in all?

1   2   3   4   5   6   7   8   9   10

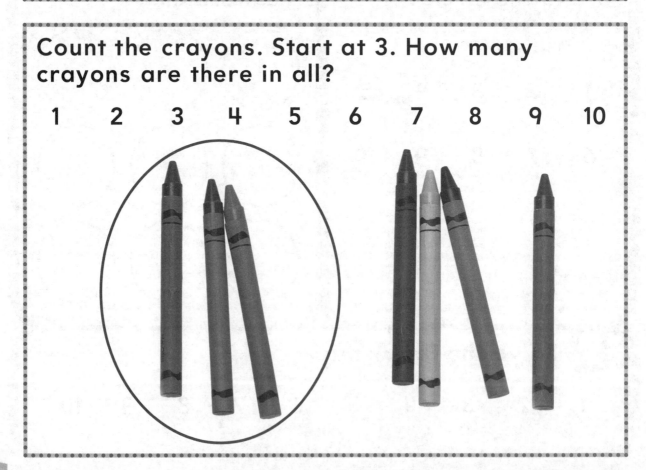

Name: _____

DIRECTIONS: Draw a picture to show the problem. Circle your answer.

Draw three more bugs. Count the bugs. Start at 3. How many bugs are there in all?

3

| 1 | 2 | 3 | 4 | 5 | 6 | 7 | 8 | 9 | 10 |

Challenge Yourself!

Name: ______________________________

DIRECTIONS: Read the problem. Solve the problem. Circle your answer.

Kimi counts her seashells. After lunch, she counts more seashells. She says, "6, 7, 8, 9, 10." How many seashells did Kimi count before lunch?

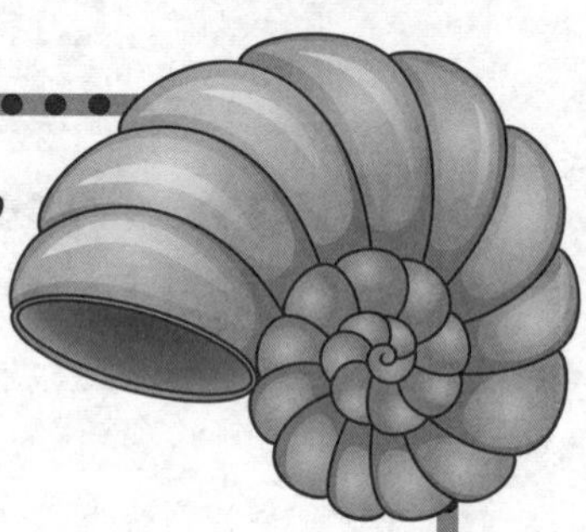

Draw a picture to show the problem.

1 2 3 4 5 6 7 8 9 10

Name: _____

 DIRECTIONS: Think about the problem.

Kenny picks 7 flowers. He picks one more. How many flowers does he have now?

Draw a picture to show the problem.

Solve It!

Name: _____

DIRECTIONS: Read the problem. Solve the problem. Circle your answer.

Problem: Tom has 4 blocks. Sue gives him 1 more. How many blocks does Tom have now?

 What Do You Know?

Draw a picture to show the problem.

 What Is Your Plan?

Count the blocks.

Solve the Problem!

1   2   3   4   5   6   7   8   9   10

Name: _____

 **DIRECTIONS:** Look at the example. Solve the problem. Circle your answer.

Picture It!

Example: Sofia has some pencils. How many pencils will there be if she gets 1 more?

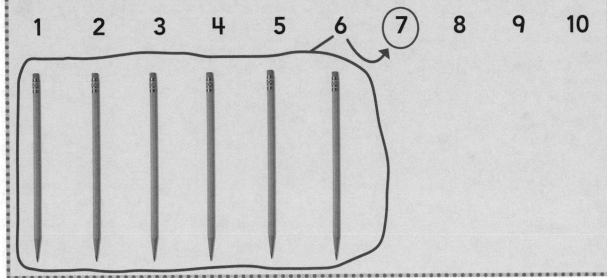

1   2   3   4   5   6   (7)   8   9   10

Ed has some fish. How many fish will there be if he gets 1 more?

1   2   3   4   5   6   7   8   9   10

Draw It!

Name: _____

DIRECTIONS: Draw a picture to show the problem. Circle your answer.

Lin has 5 pets. How many pets will she have if she gets 1 more?

| 1 | 2 | 3 | 4 | 5 | 6 | 7 | 8 | 9 | 10 |

Name: _____

 DIRECTIONS: Read the problem. Solve the problem. Circle your answers.

Challenge Yourself!

Ted has 4 toy airplanes. Luis has 1 more airplane than Ted. Dante has 1 more airplane than Luis. How many airplanes does each boy have?

Draw a picture to show the problem.

Ted: 1   2   3   4   5   6   7   8   9   10

Luis: 1   2   3   4   5   6   7   8   9   10

Dante: 1   2   3   4   5   6   7   8   9   10

Think About It!

Name: _____

DIRECTIONS: Think about the problem.

Mei has a plate with 3 strawberries. What does her plate look like?

Draw a picture to show the problem.

Name: _____

 DIRECTIONS: Read the problem. Solve the problem. Write your answer.

Problem: Tim has a dog. How many black spots does his dog have?

 What Do You Know?

Tim has a
_____
dog .

His dog has
_____
spots .

What Is Your Plan?

Count the spots. Write the numbers as you count.

1 2 3 4

 Solve the Problem!

_____

_ _ _ _ _

_____ black spots

Picture It!

Name: _____

DIRECTIONS: Look at the example. Solve the problem.

Example: Each girl has a bow. How many bows are there? Draw a bow for each girl.

Write the numbers as you count the bows.

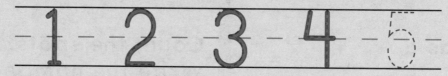

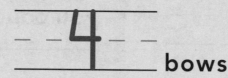

4 bows

Each boy has a hat. How many hats are there? Draw a hat for each boy.

Write the numbers as you count the hats.

1 2 3 4 5

_____ hats

#51612—180 Days of Problem Solving

Name: _____

 DIRECTIONS: Draw a picture to show the problem.

Lisa has a cat. Her cat wears a collar. The collar has 4 bells. Draw the bells.

Count the bells. Write the numbers as you count.

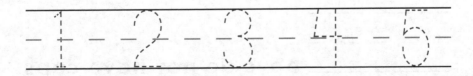

Challenge Yourself!

Name: _____

DIRECTIONS: Read the problem. Solve the problem.

How many boys have caps? How many boys do **not** have caps?

1. Count the boys who have caps. Write the numbers as you count.

$$1 \quad 2 \quad 3 \quad 4 \quad 5$$

_____

_ _ _ _ _

_____ boys have caps.

2. Count the boys who do **not** have caps. Write the numbers as you count.

$$1 \quad 2 \quad 3 \quad 4 \quad 5$$

_____

_ _ _ _ _

_____ boys do **not** have caps.

Name: _____

DIRECTIONS: Think about the problem.

Taj has 6 candles on his birthday cake. What does the cake look like?

Draw a picture to show the problem.

Solve It!

Name: _____

DIRECTIONS: Read the problem. Solve the problem. Write your answer.

Problem: Look at the fish in the tank. How many fish are there?

? **What Do You Know?**

There are ___fish___ in the tank.

What Is Your Plan?

Count the fish. Write the numbers.

_____

_____

_____

_____

_____

Solve the Problem!

_____

_____ fish

#51612—180 Days of Problem Solving

Name: _____

DIRECTIONS: Look at the example. Solve the problem.

Example: Each shirt has a pocket. How many pockets are there in all? Draw the pockets. Write the numbers as you count.

1 2 3 4 5 6 7 8 9 10

8 pockets

Each nest has a bird. How many birds are there? Draw the birds. Write the numbers as you count.

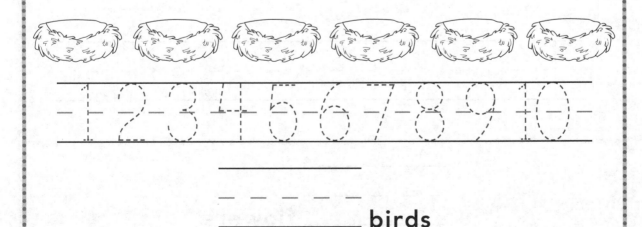

1 2 3 4 5 6 7 8 9 10

_____
_ _ _ _ _
_____ birds

Draw It!

Name: _____

DIRECTIONS: Draw a picture to show the problem. Write your answer.

Each vase has a flower. How many flowers are there in all?

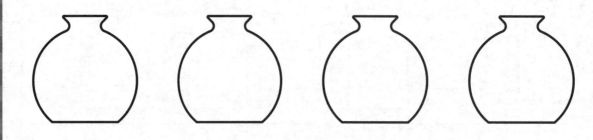

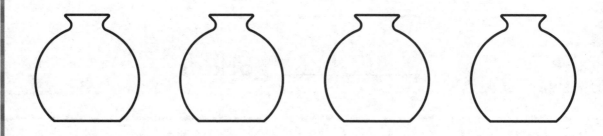

Count the flowers. Write the numbers as you count.

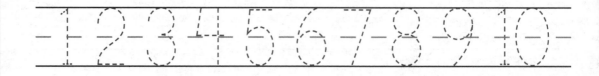

_____

_ _ _ _ _ _

_____ flowers

Name: _____

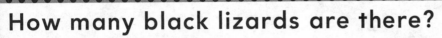 **DIRECTIONS:** Read the problem. Solve the problem.

How many black lizards are there?

Count the black lizards. Write the numbers as you count.

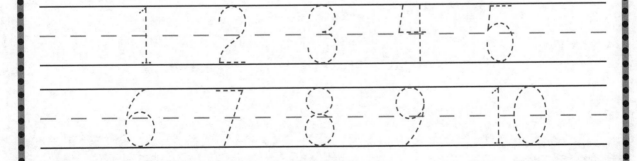

1   2   3   4   5

6   7   8   9   10

_____

_____

_____ **black lizards**

Think About It!

Name: _____

Think about the problem.

There are 19 clouds in the sky. What does the sky look like?

Draw a picture to show the problem.

Name: _____

 DIRECTIONS: Read the problem. Solve the problem.

Problem: Look at the birds in the tree. How many birds are there?

? What Do You Know?

There are 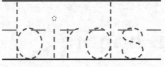 in the tree.

🔑 What Is Your Plan?

Count the birds. Write the numbers as you count.

_____

_____

_____

_____

💡 Solve the Problem!

_____

_ _ _ _ _

_____ birds

Picture It!

Name: _____

Example: Each umbrella has a handle. Draw the handles. How many handles are there?

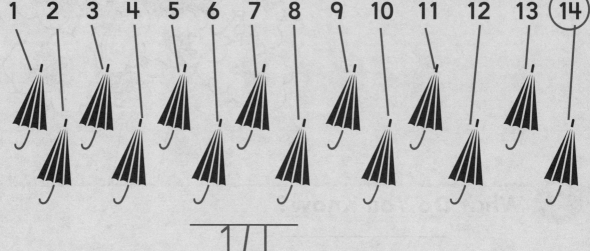

14 handles

Each squirrel has an acorn. Draw the acorns. How many acorns are there?

1 2 3 4 5 6 7 8 9 10 11 12

_____ acorns

Name: _____

Draw It!

 **DIRECTIONS:** Draw a picture to show the problem. Write your answer.

Diego put a plate on each place mat. How many plates are there in all?

Count the plates. Write the numbers as you count.

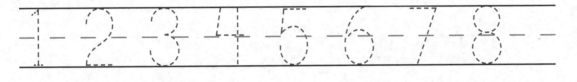

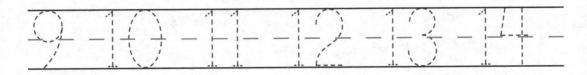

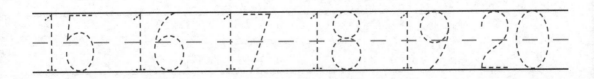

_____

- - - - -

_____ plates

Challenge Yourself!

Name: _____

DIRECTIONS: Read the problem. Solve the problem.

How many stripes does the beach towel have?

Count the stripes. Write the numbers as you count.

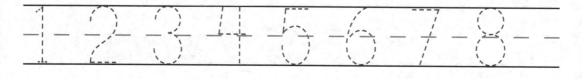

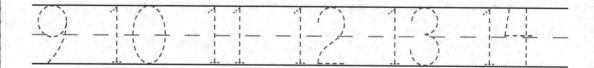

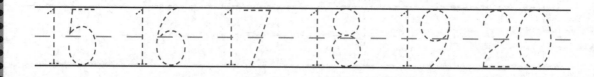

_____

- - - - -

_____ stripes

Name: _____

 DIRECTIONS: Think about the problem.

There are 10 pencils in each box. Count by tens. How many pencils are in 3 boxes?

Draw a picture to show the problem.

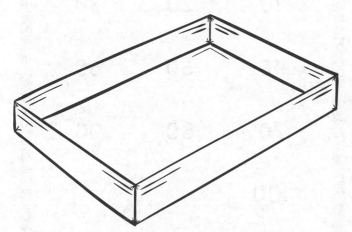

10 pencils

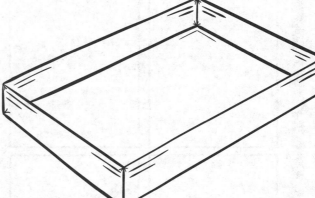

10 pencils

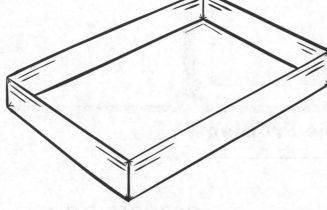

10 pencils

Solve It!

Name: _____

 DIRECTIONS: Read the problem. Solve the problem. Write your answer.

Problem: There are 10 granola bars in each box. Count by tens. How many granola bars are in 4 boxes?

? What Do You Know?

Draw a picture to show the problem.

What Is Your Plan?

Circle the numbers as you count.

10	20	30
40	50	60
70	80	90
100		

Solve the Problem!

_____

_ _ _ _ _ _ _

_____ granola bars

Name: _____

 DIRECTIONS: Look at the example. Draw lines to solve the problem. Circle your answer.

Example: Each daisy has 10 petals. Count by tens. How many petals are there in all?

| 10 | 20 | 30 | 40 | 50 | 60 | 70 | 80 | 90 | 100 |

Each hive has 10 bees. Count by tens. How many bees are there in all?

| 10 | 20 | 30 | 40 | 50 | 60 | 70 | 80 | 90 | 100 |

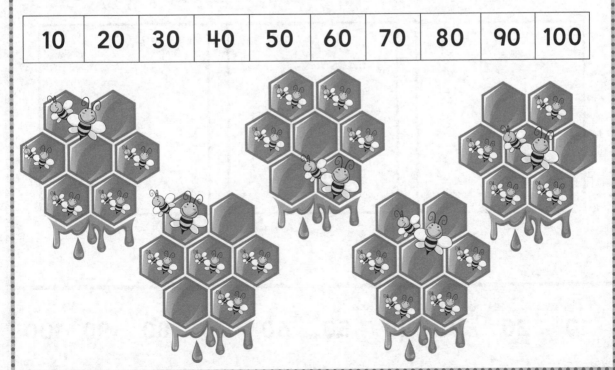

Draw It!

Name: _____

DIRECTIONS: Draw a picture to show the problem.
Circle your answer.

There are 10 oranges in each box. Count by tens. How many oranges are there in all?

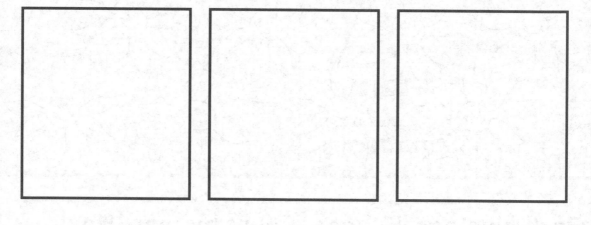

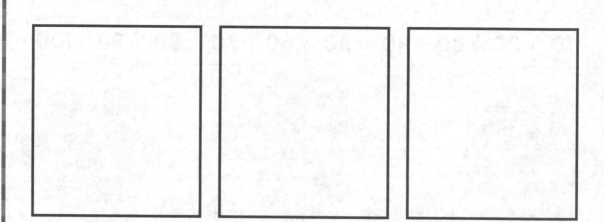

10   20   30   40   50   60   70   80   90   100

#51612—180 Days of Problem Solving

Name: _____

 DIRECTIONS: Read the problem. Solve the problem. Circle your answer.

Problem: Ali's necklace has beads. Ella's necklace has beads. Is the number of beads in each necklace equal?

Ali's necklace

Ella's necklace

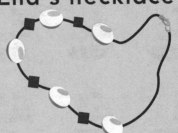

? **What Do You Know?**

What Is Your Plan?

Ali's necklace has

_____

_ _ _ _ _ _

_____ beads.

Ella's necklace has

_____

_ _ _ _ _ _

_____ beads.

Show how to compare the number of beads in each necklace.

 Solve the Problem!

Yes   **No**

Picture It!

Name: _____

DIRECTIONS: Look at the example. Draw lines to solve the problem. Circle your answer.

Example: Is the number of toy boats in each box equal?

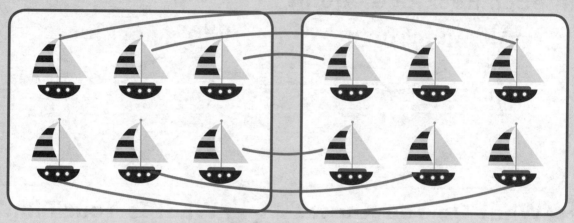

Yes   **No**

Is the number of starfish in each box equal?

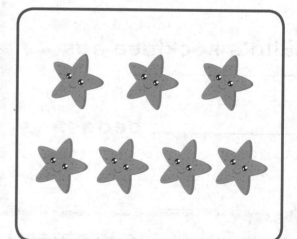

Yes   **No**

   #51612—180 Days of Problem Solving

Name: _____

DIRECTIONS: Draw a picture to show the problem. Circle your answer.

Is the number of cherries in each group equal?

Show how to compare the number of cherries in each group.

Yes   No

Challenge Yourself!

Name: _____

DIRECTIONS: Read the problem. Solve the problem.

How can you move the baseballs to make equal groups?

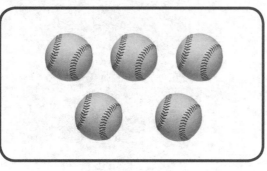

Draw a picture to show the problem.

How many baseballs are in each group now?

_____

_ _ _ _ _

_____ baseballs

#51612—180 Days of Problem Solving

Name: _____

DIRECTIONS: Think about the problem.

Which group is bigger?

Circle the group that looks bigger.

Solve It!

Name: _____

DIRECTIONS: Read the problem. Solve the problem. Circle your answer.

Problem: Which group is bigger?

palm trees

coconuts

? What Do You Know?

Count the palm trees. Write the number.

_____

_ _ _ _ _ _

_____ palm trees

Count the coconuts. Write the number.

_____

_ _ _ _ _ _

_____ coconuts

What Is Your Plan?

Show how to compare the groups.

Solve the Problem!

Name: _____

 **DIRECTIONS:** Look at the example. Draw lines to solve the problem. Circle your answer.

Picture It!

Example: Which group is bigger?

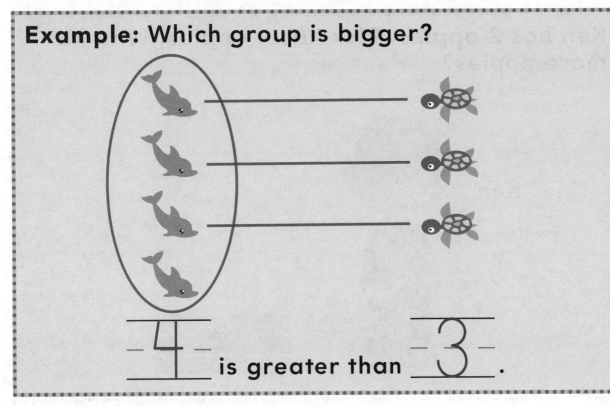

_____ is greater than __3__ .

Which group is bigger?

_____   _____

_ _ _ _ is greater than _ _ _ _ .

Draw It!

Name: _____

DIRECTIONS: Draw a picture to show the problem. Write your answer.

Ken has 2 apples. Rick has 4 apples. Who has more apples?

Ken

Rick

_____

_ _ _ _ _ _ _ _ _ _ _ _ _ _ _ _ _ _ _

_____ has more apples.

Name: _____

 DIRECTIONS: Read the problem. Solve the problem.

Write a number to make each sentence true.

1. _____ is more than  .

2. _____ is the same as  .

3. _____ is greater than  .

4. _____ is equal to  .

Think About It!

Name: _____

Think about the problem.

Which group
is smaller?

Circle the group that looks smaller.

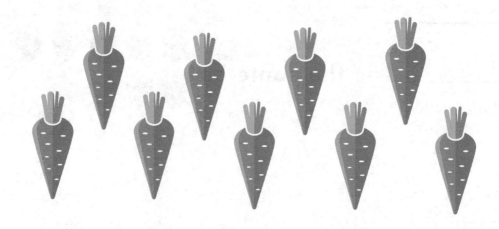

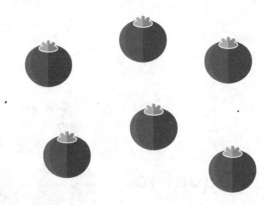

Name: _____

 DIRECTIONS: Read the problem. Solve the problem.
Circle your answer.

Solve It!

Problem: Which group is smaller?

crackers

cookies

? What Do You Know?

Count the crackers.
Write the number.

_____

‾ ‾ ‾ ‾ ‾

_____ crackers

Count the cookies.
Write the number.

_____

‾ ‾ ‾ ‾ ‾

_____ cookies

🔑 What Is Your Plan?

Show how to compare
the groups.

💡 Solve the Problem!

Picture It!

Name: _____

DIRECTIONS: Look at the example. Solve the problem. Circle your answer.

Example: Which group is smaller?

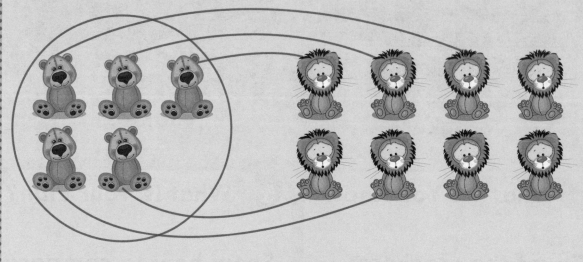

Which group is smaller?

Name: _____

Draw a picture to show the problem.
Write your answer.

Draw It!

Otis has 8 coins. Jan has 9 coins. Who has fewer coins?

Otis

Jan

_____

_ _ _ _ _ _ _ _ _ _ _ _ _ _ _

_____ has fewer coins.

Challenge Yourself!

Name: _____

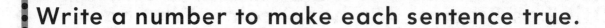

DIRECTIONS: Read the problem. Solve the problem.

Write a number to make each sentence true.

1. _____ is less than  .

2. _____ is the same as .

3. _____ is greater than  .

4. _____ is equal to .

Name: _____

DIRECTIONS: Think about the problem.

Gene has 2 animal stickers. She also has 4 plant stickers. Which group is bigger?

Draw a picture to show the problem.

Solve It!

Name: _____

 DIRECTIONS: Read the problem. Solve the problem. Write your answer.

Problem: Sid has 5 red marbles. He has 3 blue marbles. Which group is bigger?

? What Do You Know?

Draw a picture to show the problem.

🔑 What Is Your Plan?

Show how to compare 5 and 3.

💡 Solve the Problem!

_____

_ _ _ _ _ _   _ _ _ _ _ _

_____ is greater than _____ .

Name: _____

 DIRECTIONS: Look at the example. Draw lines to solve the problem. Write your answer.

Example: Binh's shirt has 1 button. Janet's shirt has 4 buttons. Which shirt has fewer buttons?

Binh's shirt   Janet's shirt

___1___ is less than ___4___ .

Sal's shirt has 2 buttons. Pam's shirt has 3 buttons. Which shirt has fewer buttons?

Sal's shirt   Pam's shirt

_____ _____

_____ is less than _____ .

Draw It!

Name: _____

DIRECTIONS: Draw a picture to show the problem. Write your answer.

Pedro has 4 grapes. Min has 2 grapes. Who has fewer grapes?

_____

_ _ _ _ _ _ _ _ _ _ _ _

_____ has fewer grapes.

#51612—180 Days of Problem Solving

Name: _____

DIRECTIONS: Read the problem. Solve the problem.

Pia has 3 cats. Saul has 1 cat. Leo has 4 cats. Who has the most cats? Who has the fewest cats?

Draw a picture to show the problem.

_____

_____ has the most cats.

_____ has the fewest cats.

Think About It!

Name: _____

DIRECTIONS: Think about the problem.

Dev has 7 green marbles. He has 10 yellow marbles. Which group is bigger?

Draw a picture to show the problem.

#51612—180 Days of Problem Solving
© Shell Education

Name: _____

 DIRECTIONS: Read the problem. Solve the problem. Write your answer.

Problem: Tia has 8 blocks. Andy has 5 blocks. Who has more?

 What Do You Know?

Draw a picture to show the problem.

What Is Your Plan?

Show how to compare 8 and 5.

 Solve the Problem!

_____

_ _ _ _ _ _ _ _ _

_____ has more blocks.

Picture It!

Name: _____

DIRECTIONS: Look at the example. Solve the problem.

Example: There are 3 bugs on a leaf. There are 9 bugs on another leaf. Which leaf has fewer bugs?

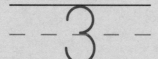 is less than ___9___ .

There are 4 bugs on a leaf. There are 6 bugs on another leaf. Which leaf has fewer bugs?

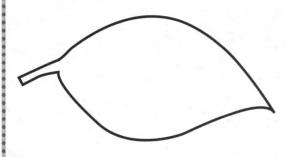 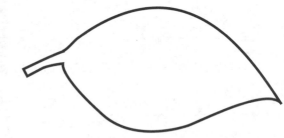

_____ is less than _____ .

Name: _____

 DIRECTIONS: Draw a picture to show the problem. Write your answer.

Jim has 5 hats. Pat has 7 hats. Who has fewer hats?

_____ _____

_____ is less than _____ .

Name: _____

DIRECTIONS: Read the problem. Solve the problem.

Write a number in each blank. Use each number only once.

| 7 | 9 | 4 | 10 | 6 | 3 | 8 | 5 |

1. _____ is greater than _____ .

2. _____ is less than _____ .

3. _____ is more than _____ .

4. _____ is less than _____ .

Name: _____

DIRECTIONS: Think about the problem.

Lola is sorting buttons. She puts big buttons in a group. She puts small buttons in a group. How many buttons are in each group?

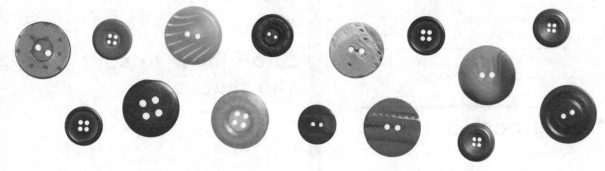

Draw a picture to show the problem.

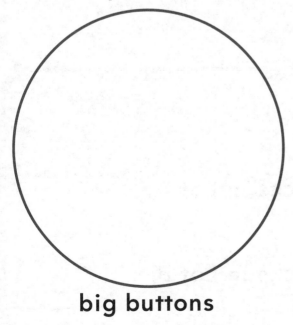

big buttons

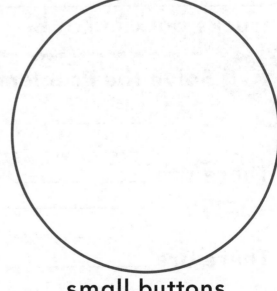

small buttons

Solve It!

Name: ______________________________

DIRECTIONS: Read the problem. Solve the problem. Write your answers.

Problem: Big trucks park in Lot A. Small trucks park in Lot B. How many trucks are in each lot?

What Do You Know?

______________ trucks park in Lot A.

______________ trucks park in Lot B.

What Is Your Plan?

Show how to sort the trucks.

Solve the Problem!

There are ______________ trucks in Lot A.

There are ______________ trucks in Lot B.

Name: _____

 DIRECTIONS: Look at the example. Draw lines to solve the problem. Write your answers.

Example: Are there more big jets or small jets?

small jets

4

big jets

2

There are more ___small___ jets.

Are there more big cars or small cars?

small cars

_____

big cars

_____

There are more _____ cars.

Draw It!

Name: _____

DIRECTIONS: Draw a picture to show the problem. Write your answers.

A farmer sorts eggs by size. How many eggs will be in each basket?

small eggs   medium eggs   large eggs

_____   _____   _____

Name: _____

DIRECTIONS: Read the problem. Solve the problem.

Kai wants to sort leaves by size.

1. How many groups should Kai make?

   _____

   _ _ _ _ _

   _____

2. Sort the leaves into groups.

3. Which group has the fewest leaves? Circle the group.

4. Which group has the most leaves? Write an X on the group.

Think About It!

Name: _____

DIRECTIONS: Think about the problem.

Ben sorts his marbles. He puts 10 blue marbles in a bag. He puts 6 orange marbles in a bag. Which bag has more?

Draw a picture to show the problem. Color the marbles.

© Shell Education

Name: _____

 DIRECTIONS: Read the problem. Solve the problem.

Solve It!

Problem: Jed sorts apples. He puts 6 red apples in a bag. He puts 4 green apples in a bag. Which bag has fewer apples?

? What Do You Know?

_____

There are _____ red apples.

_____

There are _____ green apples.

 What Is Your Plan?

Show how to sort the apples. Then, color the apples.

Solve the Problem!

_____

There are fewer _____ apples.

Picture It!

Name: _____

DIRECTIONS: Look at the example. Solve the problem. Write your answer.

Example: Emma sorts her blocks. Are there more black blocks or white blocks?

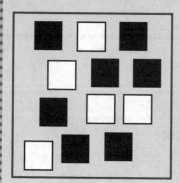

There are more  black blocks.

Jack sorts his blocks. Are there more gray blocks or white blocks?

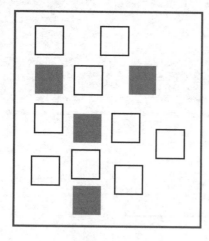

There are more _____ blocks.

#51612—180 Days of Problem Solving

Name: _____

 **DIRECTIONS:** Draw a picture to show the problem. Write your answers.

Jen sorts her rings. How many rings are in each group?

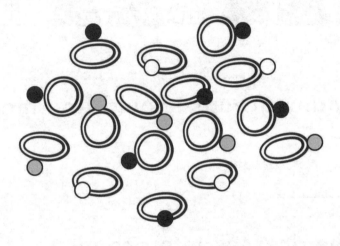

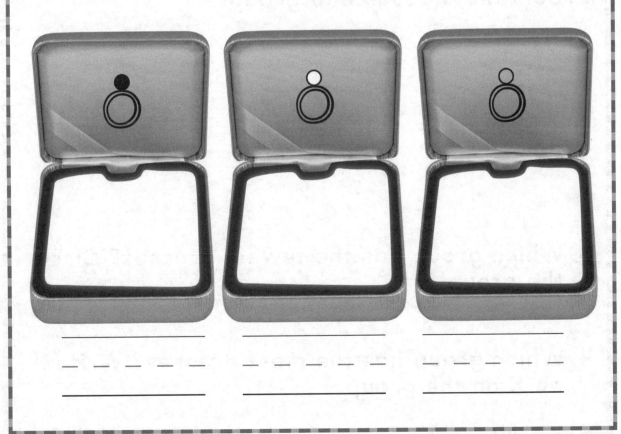

_____

_ _ _ _ _ _ _ _ _ _ _ _ _ _ _ _ _

_____

Challenge Yourself!

Name: _____

DIRECTIONS: Read the problem. Solve the problem.

Ana wants to sort her dresses by type.

1. How many groups should Ana make?

   _____

   _ _ _ _ _

   _____

2. Sort the dresses into groups.

3. Which group has the fewest dresses? Circle the group.

4. Which group has the most dresses? Write an X on the group.

Name: _____

DIRECTIONS: Think about the problem.

A craft shop sorts buttons. Sort the buttons in two groups. How many buttons are in each group?

Draw a picture to show the problem.

Name: _____

Solve It!

DIRECTIONS: Read the problem. Solve the problem.

Problem: A flower shop sorts flowers in two groups. How many flowers are in each group?

 What Do You Know?

_____

- - - - - - - - - - - - - - - - -

A flower shop sorts _____ .

_____

- - - - - - - -

The flowers are sorted in _____ groups.

🔑 **What Is Your Plan?**

Show how to sort
the flowers.

 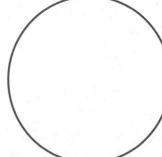

 Solve the Problem!

_____

- - - - - -

There are _____ flowers in one group.

_____

- - - - - -

There are _____ flowers in the other group.

 #51612—180 Days of Problem Solving

Name: _____

 DIRECTIONS: Look at the example. Solve the problem.

Example: Sort the hats two different ways.

Sort the fish two different ways.

 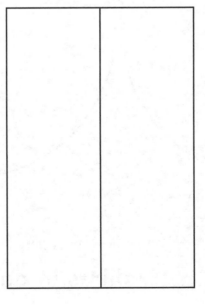 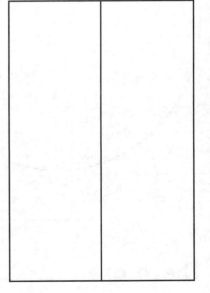

Draw It!

Name: _____

DIRECTIONS: Draw a picture to show the problem.

A store wants to sort these shirts. Sort the shirts in two groups. How many shirts are in each group?

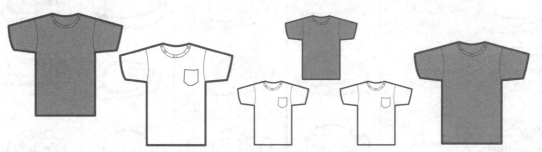

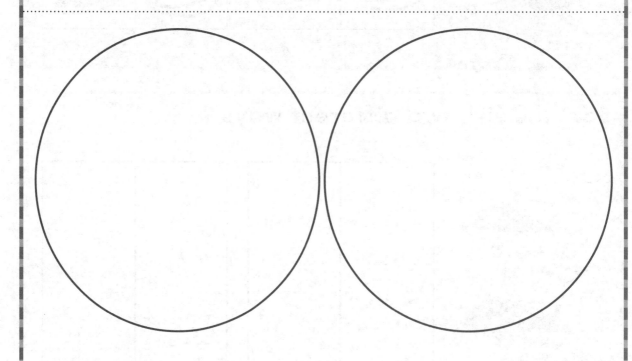

There are _____ shirts in one group.

There are _____ shirts in the other group.

Name: _____

 DIRECTIONS: Read the problem. Solve the problem.

Color the hearts three different colors.

1. Sort the hearts in three groups.

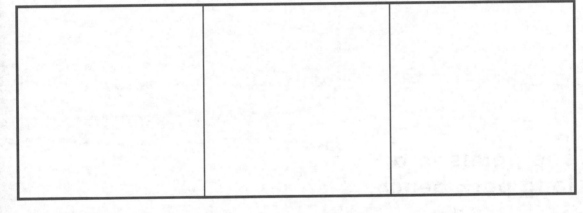

2. Sort the hearts a different way.

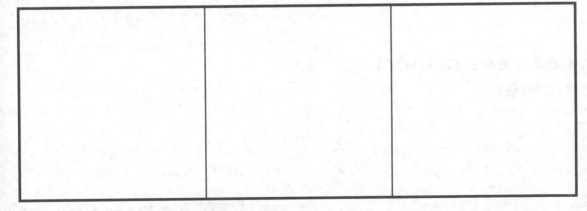

Think About It!

Name: _____

DIRECTIONS: Think about the problem.

Lee is at the park. What does she see? Draw what she sees.

1. Lee says, "I see a tall tree."

2. Lee points to a long park bench.

3. Lee sees a short flower.

Name: _____

 DIRECTIONS: Read the problem. Solve the problem.
Circle your answers.

Problem: Allen has a crayon. He has a book.
Are these objects light or heavy?

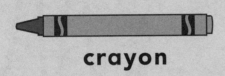
crayon

book

 What Do You Know?

_____
- - - - - - - - - - - - - - - - - - -
Allen has a _____.

_____
- - - - - - - - - - - - - - - - - - -
Allen has a _____.

What Is Your Plan?

Hold a crayon.

Hold a book.

 Solve the Problem!

The crayon is   light   heavy.

The book is   light   heavy.

Picture It!

Name: _____

DIRECTIONS: Look at the example. Solve the problem. Circle your answers.

Example: Conni has a ladder. Describe the ladder.

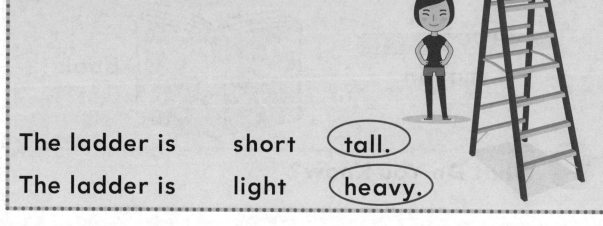

The ladder is   short   (tall.)
The ladder is   light   (heavy.)

1. Jesse has a truck. Describe the truck.

The truck is   short   long.

The truck is   light   heavy.

2. Amanda has a baby chick. Describe the chick.

The chick is   short   long.

The chick is   light   heavy.

Name: _____

 DIRECTIONS: Draw a picture to show the problem.

Jung has many pets. He has a long snake. He has a short bird. He has a heavy dog. What do his pets look like?

snake

bird

dog

Name: _____

Read the problem. Solve the problem.

Challenge Yourself!

1. Draw an object that is long and light.

2. Draw an object that is short and heavy.

3. Draw an object that is long and heavy.

4. Draw an object that is short and light.

#51612—180 Days of Problem Solving © Shell Education

Name: _____

DIRECTIONS: Think about the problem.

Jack is describing objects. Draw a picture to compare the objects.

1. Jack says, "The building is taller than the house."

2. Jack says, "The worm is shorter than the snake."

3. Jack says, "The car is heavier than the bike."

Solve It!

Name: _____

DIRECTIONS: **Read the problem. Solve the problem.**

Problem: Kimi has a pencil. Her friend has a crayon. Which object is longer?

crayon

pencil

❓ What Do You Know?

_____

Kimi has a _____.

_____

Her friend has a _____.

🔑 What Is Your Plan?

Compare the lengths of the objects.

💡 Solve the Problem!

_____

The _____ is longer.

Name: _____

 DIRECTIONS: Look at the example. Solve the problem.

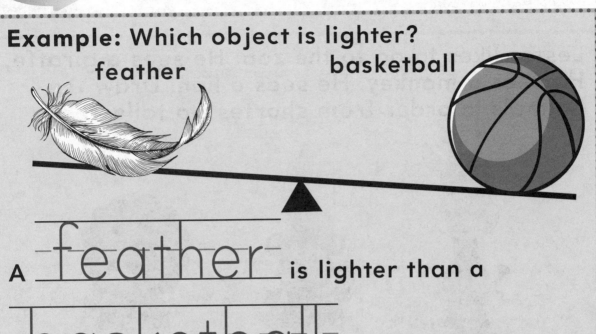

Example: Which object is lighter?

feather   basketball

A ___feather___ is lighter than a

___basketball___ .

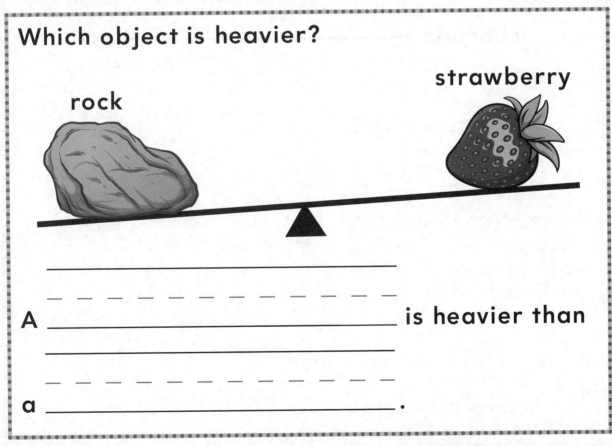

Which object is heavier?

rock   strawberry

A _____ is heavier than

a _____ .

Draw It!

Name: _____

DIRECTIONS: Draw a picture to show the problem.

Lester likes to go to the zoo. He sees a giraffe. He sees a monkey. He sees a lion. Draw the animals in order from shortest to tallest.

giraffe   monkey   lion

shortest ⟶ tallest

Name: _____

 DIRECTIONS: Read the problem. Solve the problem.

1. Draw two objects. Show that one object is longer.

2. Draw two objects. Show that one object is heavier.

3. Draw two objects. Show that one object is shorter.

4. Draw two objects. Show that one object is lighter.

Name: _____

DIRECTIONS: Think about the problem.

Two ducks swim in a pond. Two more ducks come to swim. How many ducks are in the pond now?

Draw a picture to show the problem.

Name: _____

 DIRECTIONS: Read the problem. Solve the problem.

Problem: There are 3 cows in a barn. There is 1 horse in the barn. How many animals are in the barn?

 What Do You Know?

_____

There are _____ cows.

_____

There is _____ horse.

What Is Your Plan?

Draw a picture to show the problem.

 Solve the Problem!

_____

_____ animals

Name: _____

DIRECTIONS: Look at the example. Draw a picture to show the problem. Write your answer.

Picture It!

Example: Paki has 3 balloons. He gets 2 more. How many balloons does he have now?

Paki has __5__ balloons.

Jada has 1 goldfish. She gets 2 more. How many goldfish does she have now?

Jada has _____ goldfish.

#51612—180 Days of Problem Solving

Name: _____

 **DIRECTIONS:** Draw a picture to show the problem. Write your answer.

A vase has 2 red flowers and 3 yellow flowers. How many flowers are in the vase?

_____

There are _____ flowers.

Challenge Yourself!

Name: ____________________

DIRECTIONS: Read the problem. Solve the problem.

Kiki has 4 dresses. Two are green and the rest are red. How many red dresses does Kiki have?

Draw a picture to show the problem.

____

Kiki has ____________ red dresses.

Name: _____

DIRECTIONS: Think about the problem.

Three birds are on a tree branch. Four more birds land on the branch. How many birds are on the branch now?

Draw a picture to show the problem.

Solve It!

Name: _____

DIRECTIONS: Read the problem. Solve the problem.

Problem: Four bunnies hop to a tree. Five more bunnies hop to the tree. How many bunnies are there now?

? What Do You Know?

Draw a picture to show the problem.

What Is Your Plan?

Count the bunnies. Write the numbers.

_____

_ _ _ _ _ _ _ _ _ _ _ _ _ _ _ _

_____

Solve the Problem!

_____

_ _ _ _ _ _ _

_____ bunnies

Name: _____

 DIRECTIONS: Look at the example. Solve the problem.

Example: There are 3 chicks in the yard. Six more chicks come. How many chicks are in the yard now?

There are _____9_____ chicks.

There are 5 kittens playing in the grass. One more kitten comes to play. How many kittens are playing in the grass now?

There are _____ kittens.

Name: _____

Draw It!

DIRECTIONS: Draw a picture to show the problem. Write your answer.

A hen lays eggs in a nest. There are 7 brown eggs and 3 white eggs. How many eggs are in the nest?

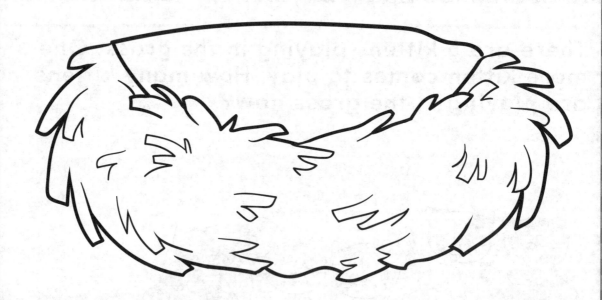

_____

_ _ _ _ _

_____ **eggs**

Name: _____

 DIRECTIONS: Read the problem. Solve the problem.

Tia picks 8 flowers. Six are yellow and the rest are pink. How many pink flowers does Tia pick?

Draw a picture to show the problem.

Tia picks _____ pink flowers.

Think About It!

Name: _____

DIRECTIONS: Think about the problem.

There are 2 puppies playing. Four more puppies come to play. How many puppies are playing now?

Draw a picture to solve the problem.

Name: _____

 DIRECTIONS: Read the problem. Solve the problem.

Problem: There is 1 red bug on a leaf. Eight green bugs crawl onto the leaf. How many bugs are on the leaf now?

? **What Do You Know?**

Draw a picture to show the problem.

What Is Your Plan?

Write a number sentence to show the problem.

_____ + _____ = _____

Solve the Problem!

_____ bugs

Picture It!

Name: _____

DIRECTIONS: Look at the example. Draw a picture to solve the problem. Write your answer.

Example: Mr. Lin has books on his desk. There are 5 big books and 4 small books. How many books are on his desk?

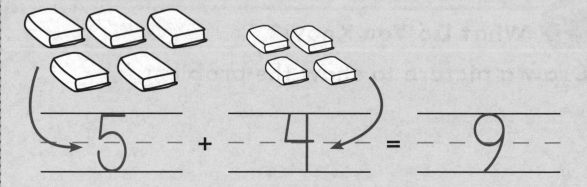

$$5 + 4 = 9$$

Mr. Lin has ___9___ books.

Mrs. Perez has pens on her desk. There are 4 blue pens and 3 red pens. How many pens are on her desk?

_____ + _____ = _____

_____

Mrs. Perez has _____ pens.

Name: _____

 DIRECTIONS: Draw a picture to show the problem. Write your answer.

Leah has 10 hair bows. Six are red and the rest are pink. How many pink bows does she have?

Draw It!

6 + _ _ _ _ _ _ = 10

_____

_ _ _ _ _

_____ pink bows

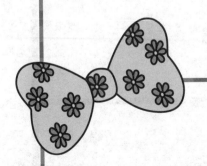

© Shell Education

#51612—180 Days of Problem Solving

121

Challenge Yourself!

Name: _____

DIRECTIONS: Read the problem. Solve the problem.

There are 8 frogs on a log. Two frogs are green. One frog is orange. The rest of the frogs are red. How many frogs are red?

Draw a picture to show the problem.

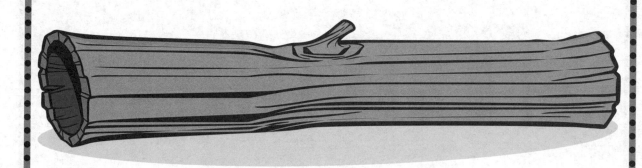

$$2 + 1 + \underline{} = 8$$

There are _____ red frogs.

© Shell Education

Name: _____

DIRECTIONS: Think about the problem.

Jon has a basket of 5 apples. There are red apples. There are green apples. How many ways can you use red and green apples to fill his basket?

Color the apples to show all the ways to fill the basket.

Solve It!

Name: _____

 DIRECTIONS: Read the problem. Solve the problem.

Problem: There are 3 crayons in a box. Some are blue. Some are black. How many ways can you use blue and black crayons to fill the box?

? What Do You Know?

_____

There are _____ crayons in the box.

Some are _____ crayons.

Some are _____ crayons.

What Is Your Plan?

Draw a picture to show all the ways to fill the box.

Solve the Problem!

_____ _____

_____ blue crayons and _____ black crayon

_____ _____

_____ blue crayon and _____ black crayons

Name: _____

 DIRECTIONS: Look at the example. Solve the problem.

Example: Draw dots to show how many parts make up the whole. Write a number sentence for each model.

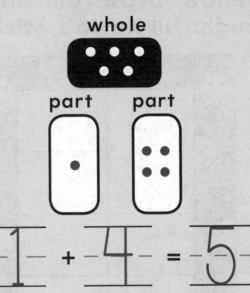

whole

part   part

$2 + 3 = 5$

whole

part   part

$1 + 4 = 5$

Draw dots to show how many parts make up the whole. Write a number sentence for each model.

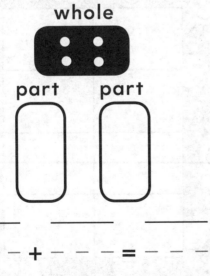

whole

part   part

___ + ___ = ___

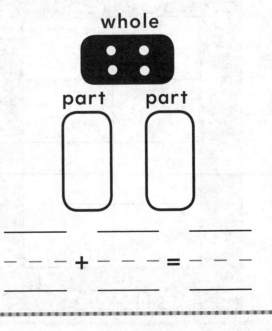

whole

part   part

___ + ___ = ___

Name: _____

Draw It!

DIRECTIONS: Draw a picture to show the problem.

Kevin has 8 happy face stickers on his sticker chart. Some stickers are red and some are yellow. Draw four different ways the stickers might fill Kevin's sticker chart.

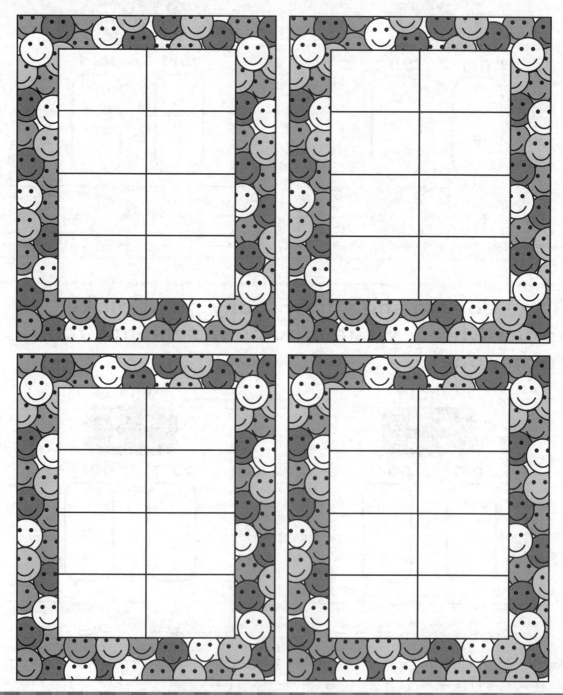

Name: _____

 DIRECTIONS: Read the problem. Solve the problem.

Jade has 7 grapes in a snack bag. Some grapes are purple and some are green.

Draw all of the ways to make 7 grapes in the snack bag.

Think About It!

Name: _____

DIRECTIONS: Think about the problem.

A full box of crayons has 10 crayons. Maya has 4 crayons. How many crayons are missing?

Draw a picture to show the problem.

Name: _____

 DIRECTIONS: Read the problem. Solve the problem.

Problem: A full box of markers has 10 markers. Jay has 7 markers in his box. How many markers are missing?

 What Do You Know?

_____

- - - - - - - -

A full box has _____ markers.

_____

- - - - - -

Jay has _____ markers.

 What Is Your Plan?

Draw a picture to show how to make a full box of markers.

Solve the Problem!

_____

- - - - - -

_____ markers

Picture It!

Name: _____

DIRECTIONS: Look at the example. Solve the problem.

Example: A box holds 10 pencils. Sue has 3 pencils. She wants to fill the box. How many more pencils does she need?

7 pencils

A box holds 10 plums. Mike has 6 plums. He wants to fill the box. How many more plums does he need?

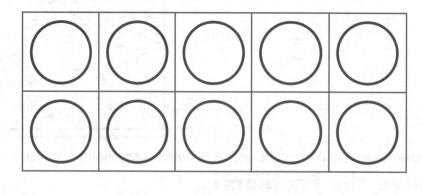

_____ plums

Name: _____

 DIRECTIONS: Solve the problem using a ten frame. Write your answer.

Deb likes to wear rings. She has 10 rings. She puts 8 in a box. How many rings is she wearing?

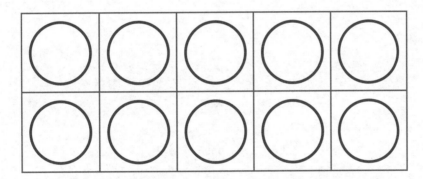

_____

_ _ _ _ _

_____ rings

Name: _____

DIRECTIONS: Read the problem. Solve the problem.

Kali has 10 pens. She has 2 more blue pens than green pens. How many blue pens does she have? How many green pens does she have?

Draw a picture to show the problem.

Kali has _____ blue pens.

Kali has _____ green pens.

#51612—180 Days of Problem Solving

Name: _____

DIRECTIONS: Think about the problem.

Three birds are in a nest. One bird flies away. How many birds are in the nest now?

Draw a picture to show the problem.

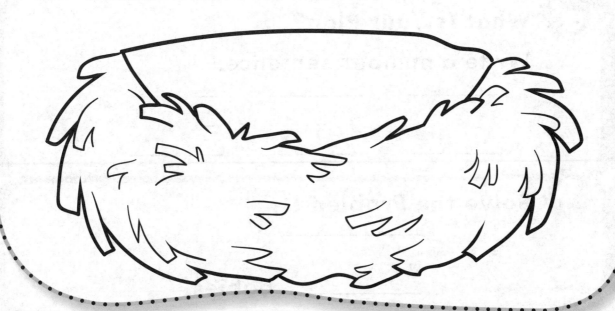

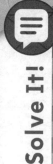

Solve It!

Name: _____

Read the problem. Solve the problem.

Problem: Four babies are playing on the rug. Two babies crawl away. How many babies are on the rug now?

? What Do You Know?

Draw a picture to show the problem.

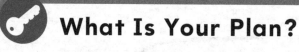

🔑 What Is Your Plan?

Write a number sentence.

_____   _____   _____

_ _ _ _   − _ _ _ _   = _ _ _ _

_____   _____   _____

💡 Solve the Problem!

_____

_ _ _ _ _

_____ babies

Name: _____

 DIRECTIONS: Look at the example. Solve the problem.

Example: There are 5 cherries in a bowl. Pete eats 2 cherries. How many cherries are in the bowl now?

$$5 - 2 = 3$$

___3___ cherries

There are 3 peaches in a basket. Dora eats 1 peach. How many peaches are in the basket now?

_____ - _____ = _____

_____

_____ peaches

Draw It!

Name: _____

DIRECTIONS: Draw a picture to show the problem. Write your answer.

Nick has 5 toy cars. He gives 3 toy cars to his friends. How many toy cars does Nick have now?

_____

_____ toy cars

#51612—180 Days of Problem Solving

Name: _____

 DIRECTIONS: Read the problem. Solve the problem.

There are 4 slices of pizza in a box. Tom eats 2 slices. Maria eats 1 slice. How many slices of pizza are in the box now?

Draw a picture to show the problem.

_____ slice of pizza

Think About It!

Name: _____

DIRECTIONS: Think about the problem.

There are 9 cars in a parking lot. Four cars drive away. How many cars are in the parking lot now?

Draw a picture to show the problem.

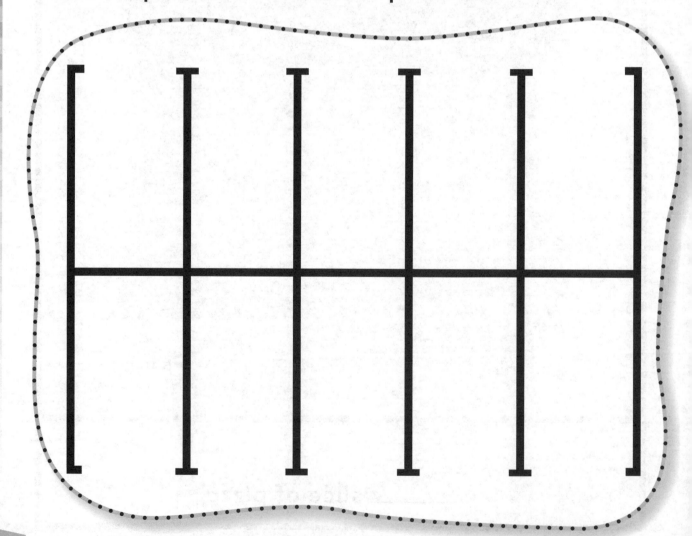

Name: _____

 DIRECTIONS: Read the problem. Solve the problem.

Problem: There are 8 boats at a dock. Five boats sail away. How many boats are at the dock now?

? What Do You Know?

Draw a picture to show the problem.

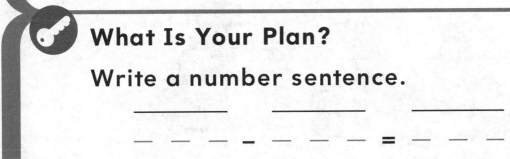

What Is Your Plan?

Write a number sentence.

_____ _____ _____

__ __ __ - __ __ __ = _____

_____ _____ _____

 Solve the Problem!

_____

__ __ __ __ __

_____ boats

Picture It!

Name: _____

DIRECTIONS: Look at the example. Solve the problem.

Example: There are 10 kids playing at the playground. Three kids go home. How many kids are still playing?

10 - 3 = 7

7 kids

There are 7 dogs at the park. Five dogs go home. How many dogs are still at the park?

_____ - _____ = _____

_____

_____ dogs

Name: _____

 DIRECTIONS: Draw a picture to show the problem. Write your answer.

There are 10 hot air balloons. Six hot air balloons fly away. How many hot air balloons are left?

_____

_ _ _ _ _

_____ hot air balloons

Challenge Yourself!

Name: _____

DIRECTIONS: Read the problem. Solve the problem.

Mita has 9 balloons. Three are red. Three are yellow. The rest are blue. How many are blue?

Draw a picture to show the problem.

_____

_ _ _ _ _

_____ blue balloons

Name: _____

DIRECTIONS: Think about the problem.

There are 6 sheep in a barn. Two sheep go outside. How many sheep are left?

Draw a picture to show the problem.

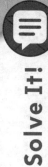

Solve It!

Name: _____

DIRECTIONS: Read the problem. Solve the problem.

Problem: There are 10 cows in a field. Five cows go into a barn. How many cows are still in the field?

? **What Do You Know?**

Draw a picture to show the problem.

🔑 **What Is Your Plan?**

Write a number sentence.

_____ _____ _____

___ ___ ___ - ___ ___ ___ = ___ ___ ___

_____ _____ _____

💡 **Solve the Problem!**

_____

___ ___ ___ ___ ___

_____ cows

Name: _____

 DIRECTIONS: Look at the example. Solve the problem.

Picture It!

Example: There are 6 birds in a tree. Two birds fly away. How many birds are left?

6 - 2 = 4

4 birds

There are 7 ducks in the pond. Three ducks swim away. How many ducks are left?

___ - ___ = ___

___ ducks

Draw It!

Name: _____

DIRECTIONS: Draw a picture to solve the problem. Then, write a number sentence.

There are 8 butterflies on a bush. Two butterflies fly away. How many butterflies are left?

_____ _____ _____

__ __ __ - __ __ __ = __ __ __

_____ _____ _____

_____

__ __ __ __ __ **butterflies**

Name: _____

 **DIRECTIONS:** Read the problem. Solve the problem.

There are 10 hens. Two hens are in the yard. Three hens are in the coop. How many hens are in the barn?

1. Draw a picture to show the problem.

2. Write a number sentence to solve the problem.

_____ _____ _____ _____

_ _ _ _ – _ _ _ _ – _ _ _ _ = _ _ _ _

_____ _____ _____

3. Write your answer.

_____

_ _ _ _ _ _

There are _____ hens in the barn.

Think About It!

Name: _____

DIRECTIONS: Think about the problem.

Mary has some beads. How many beads does she have?

Color the ten frames to show the problem.

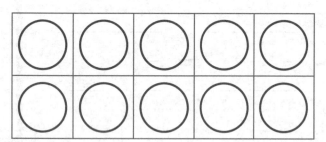
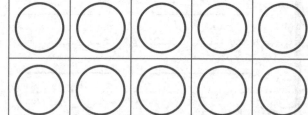

#51612—180 Days of Problem Solving

Name: _____

 DIRECTIONS: Read the problem. Solve the problem.

Problem: Phil has hats for his birthday party. How many hats does Phil have?

? **What Do You Know?**

_____

– – – – – –

Phil has _____ for his birthday party.

What Is Your Plan?

Color the ten frames to show the problem.

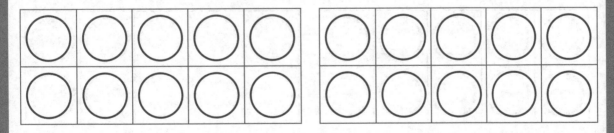

Solve the Problem!

_____

– – – – – –

_____ hats

Name: _____

DIRECTIONS: Look at the example. Solve the problem.

Picture It!

Example: Kate sells 10 cakes at a bake sale. Will sells 8 cakes. How many cakes do they sell in all?

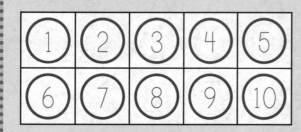 

$$10 + 8 = 18$$

$$18 \text{ cakes}$$

Jake makes 10 cards. Simon makes 5 cards. How many cards do they make in all?

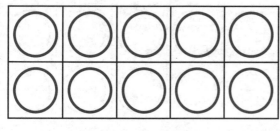 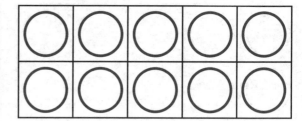

$$10 + \underline{\quad} = \underline{\quad}$$

$$\underline{\qquad} \text{ cards}$$

Name: _____

 DIRECTIONS: Solve the problem with the ten frames. Write your answer.

Dan bakes 10 cookies. He bakes 7 more. How many cookies does he bake in all?

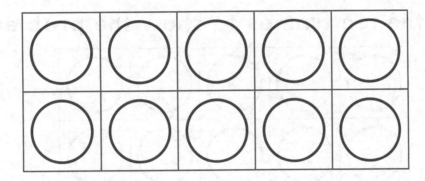

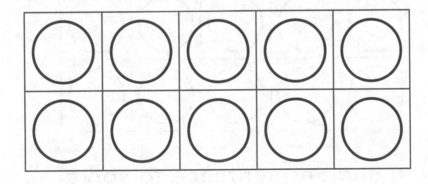

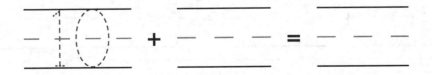

_____ _____ _____
10 + _____ = _____

_____

_____ cookies

Challenge Yourself!

Name: _____

DIRECTIONS: Read the problem. Solve the problem.

Carrie has 10 books on her shelf. Her mom gives her 2 more books. Her dad gives her 7 more books. How many books does Carrie have now?

1. Use the ten frames to show the problem.

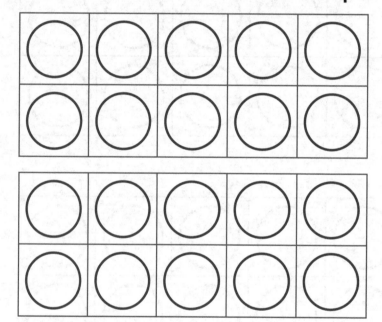

2. Write a number sentence to solve the problem.

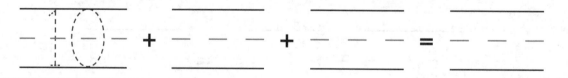

3. Write your answer.

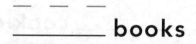

_____ books

Name: _____

 DIRECTIONS: Think about the problem.

Mary finds 16 seashells at the beach. She makes a group of 10 seashells. How many shells are left over?

Draw a picture to show the problem.

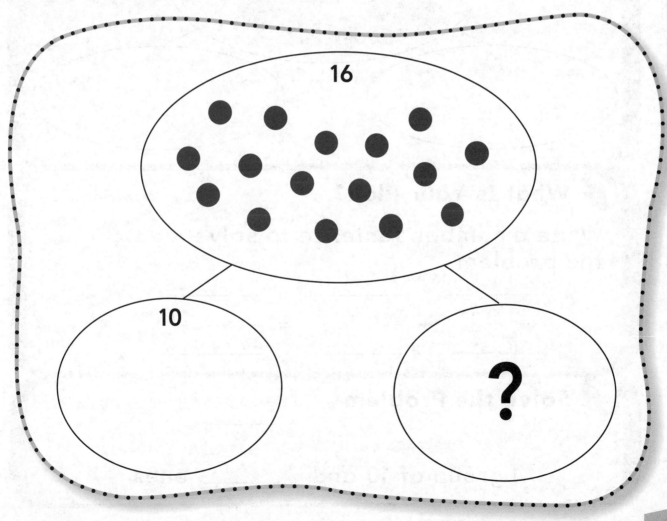

16

10

?

Solve It!

Name: _____

Read the problem. Solve the problem.

Problem: Gino has 13 pennies in his piggy bank. He makes a group of 10 pennies. How many are left over?

? What Do You Know?

Draw a picture to show the problem.

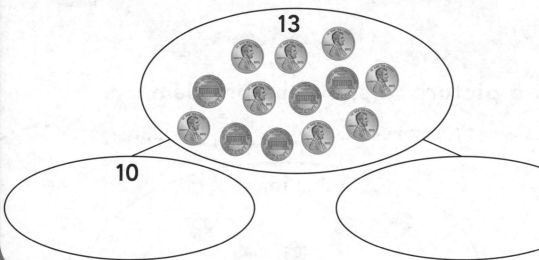

What Is Your Plan?

Write a number sentence to solve the problem.

10 + _____ _____ = _____ _____

Solve the Problem!

_____

_ _ _

1 group of 10 and _____ ones

Name: _____

DIRECTIONS: Look at the example. Solve the problem.

Example: Patty has 12 limes. She puts 10 limes in a bag. How many limes are left over?

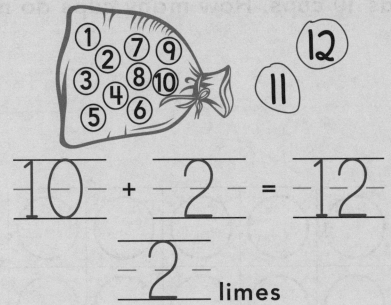

$$10 + 2 = 12$$

$$\underline{2}\ \text{limes}$$

Saul has 14 lemons. He puts 10 lemons in a bag. How many lemons are left over?

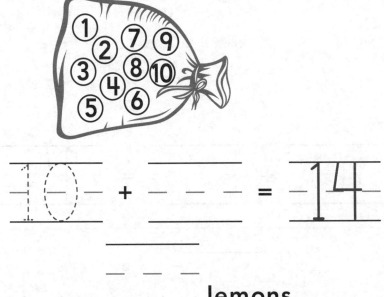

$$10 + \underline{} = 14$$

_____ lemons

Draw It!

Name: _____

DIRECTIONS: Solve the problem with the ten frame. Write your answer.

There are 14 cups of punch for a party. The tray holds 10 cups. How many cups do not fit?

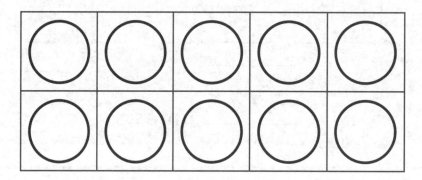

10 + ____ = 14

_____ cups

Name: _____

 DIRECTIONS: Read the problem. Solve the problem.

Ray puts 18 pancakes on 3 plates. The first plate has 10 pancakes. The next plate has 3 pancakes. How many pancakes are on the last plate?

1. Draw a picture to show the problem.

2. Write a number sentence to solve the problem.

_10_ + _____ + _____ = _18_

3. Write your answer.

There are _____ pancakes on the last plate.

Think About It!

Name: _____

DIRECTIONS: **Think about the problem.**

Brett says his mom's cell phone is a rectangle. Is he correct?

Circle the rectangles.

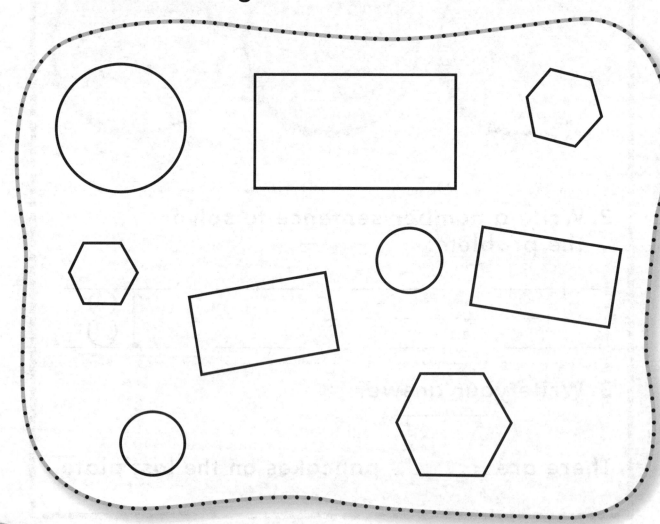

 #51612—180 Days of Problem Solving

Name: _____

 DIRECTIONS: Read the problem. Solve the problem. Circle your answer.

Problem: Kelly says her sandwich is a square. Do you agree with her?

 What Do You Know?

_____

A square has _____ equal sides.

A square has _____ corners.

🔑 **What Is Your Plan?**

Compare Kelly's sandwich to what you know about squares.

💡 **Solve the Problem!**

Yes   No

Picture It!

Name: _____

Look at the example. Solve the problem.

Example: Mark says this shape is a triangle. Is he correct?

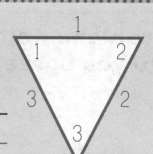

How many sides are there? __3__

How many angles are there? __3__

Is Mark correct? Circle your answer.

(Yes)   No

Kathy says this shape is a triangle. Is she correct?

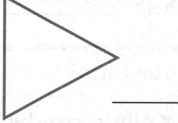

How many sides are there? _____

How many angles are there? _____

Is Kathy correct? Circle your answer.

Yes   No

#51612—180 Days of Problem Solving

Name: _____

 **DIRECTIONS:** Draw the shapes. Write the number of angles.

Shape	Sides	Angles
▢	4	
	3	3
	0	0
⬡	6	

Name: _____

DIRECTIONS: Read the problem. Solve the problem.

Draw a picture of a pig using these shapes:

- a circle for the head

- 2 small triangles for the ears

- a rectangle for the body

- 4 small squares for the feet

- a small hexagon for the nose

- 2 small circles for the eyes

Name: _____

DIRECTIONS Think about the problem.

Abby says that all squares and rectangles have 4 sides and 4 corners. Is she correct?

Circle the squares and rectangles. Draw an X on the shapes that are **not** squares or rectangles.

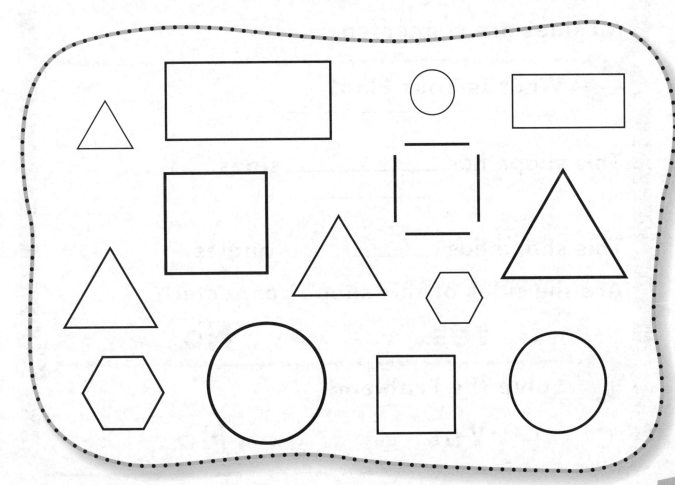

Solve It!

Name: _____

DIRECTIONS: Read the problem. Solve the problem. Circle your answer.

Problem: Tony says this shape is a triangle. Is he correct?

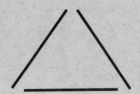

 What Do You Know?

_____

A triangle has _____ sides.

_____

A triangle has _____ angles.

All sides are connected.

What Is Your Plan?

_____

This shape has _____ sides.

_____

This shape has _____ angles.

Are the sides of this shape connected?

Yes   **No**

 Solve the Problem!

Yes   **No**

Name: _____

 **DIRECTIONS:** Look at the example. Draw a picure to solve the problem. Write your answer.

Picture It!

Example: Pete draws a square. Lara draws a hexagon. Which shape has more sides?

square

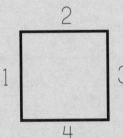

hexagon

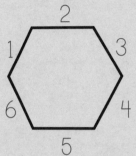

A ___hexagon___ has more sides than a

___square___ .

Randy draws a rectangle. Vickie draws a triangle. Which shape has more sides?

rectangle   triangle

A _____ has more sides than a

_____ .

Name: _____

DIRECTIONS: Draw a picture to show the shape.

Draw It!

1. Draw a triangle two different ways.

2. Draw two different shapes that have 4 sides and 4 corners.

Name: _____

 DIRECTIONS: Read the problem. Solve the problem.

Draw a picture of a dog with these shapes:

- 2 triangles

- 3 rectangles

- 1 square

- Draw 2 eyes using a shape with 0 angles.

- Draw the tail using a shape with 2 long sides and 2 short sides.

Think About It!

Name: _____

Think about the problem.

Billy has 2 squares. Can he make a rectangle with these squares?

Draw a line on each rectangle to show two squares.

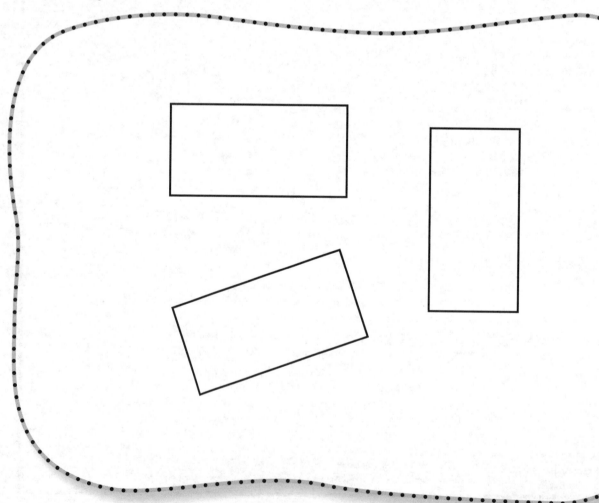

Name: _____

 DIRECTIONS: Read the problem. Solve the problem.

Problem: Serena has 2 triangles. Can she make a square with these triangles?

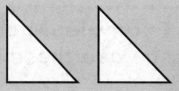

? What Do You Know?

A triangle has _____ sides.

A triangle has _____ angles.

A square has _____ equal sides.

A square has _____ corners.

⚷ What Is Your Plan?

Draw a square.

How can you draw a line on your square to show the two triangles?

💡 Solve the Problem!

Yes   No

Picture It!

Name: _____

DIRECTIONS: Look at the example. Solve the problem.

Example: Michelle has these shapes. How can she use these shapes to make a flower?

Terrell has these shapes. How can he use these shapes to make a house?

 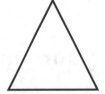

Name: _____

 DIRECTIONS: How many triangles do you need to make each shape? Draw lines to show the triangles.

Example

_____2_____ triangles

1.

_____ triangles

2.

_____ triangles

3.

_____ triangles

Challenge Yourself!

Name: _____

DIRECTIONS: Read the problem. Solve the problem.

What shapes can you make with triangles?

1. Draw a shape using triangles.

2. Can you make another shape using triangles?

3. Can you make a third shape using triangles?

Name: _____

  Think about the problem.

Eddie draws a picture with shapes. He draws a house next to a tree.

What shapes might Eddie use to draw his picture?

Name: _____

Solve It!

Read the problem. Solve the problem.

Problem: Sally draws a picture with shapes. She draws 4 triangles, 3 rectangles, and 2 squares. What might her picture look like?

? What Do You Know?

Draw a triangle.

Draw a rectangle.

Draw a square.

🔑 What Is Your Plan?

_____

I need to draw _____ triangles.

_____

I need to draw _____ rectangles.

_____

I need to draw _____ squares.

 Solve the Problem!

Name: _____

 DIRECTIONS: Look at the example. Solve the problem. Circle your answers.

Example: Julio draws this picture.

He says he drew a triangle for the roof of the house. Is he correct?   (Yes)   No

He says the sun is below the car. Is he correct?   Yes   (No)

He says he drew a triangle and a rectangle for the tree. Is he correct?   Yes   No

He says he drew a circle and six rectangles for the sun. Is he correct?   Yes   No

He says the windows are above the door. Is he correct?   Yes   No

He says the car is in front of the house. Is he correct?   Yes   No

Name: _____

DIRECTIONS: Draw a picture to show the shapes.

James tells his friend to draw these shapes:

- a square next to a rectangle

- a triangle below the rectangle

- a circle above the rectangle

- a rectangle beside the triangle

What does his picture look like?

Name: _____

 DIRECTIONS: Read the problem. Solve the problem.

Draw a picture using these shapes:

     1 circle   1 triangle   1 rectangle

Use the words to complete the sentences.

     beside   above   below

_____

My rectangle is _____ my triangle.

_____

My circle is _____ my rectangle.

_____

My triangle is _____ my circle.

Think About It!

Name: _____

DIRECTIONS: Think about the problem.

Ana says her basketball is a sphere. Is she correct?

Circle the spheres.

#51612—180 Days of Problem Solving   © Shell Education

Name: _____

Solve It!

 DIRECTIONS: Read the problem. Solve the problem. Circle your answer.

Problem: Joe says his hat is a cone. Do you agree with him?

 What Do You Know?

Draw a cone.

 What Is Your Plan?

Compare Joe's hat to your drawing.

Solve the Problem!

Yes   No

Picture It!

Name: _____

DIRECTIONS:
Look at the example. Solve the problem.

Example: What flat shape do you see in the cylinder?

cylinder

Draw the shape.

Name the shape.

circle

What flat shape do you see in the cube?

cube

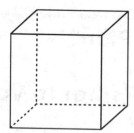

Draw the shape.

Name the shape.

#51612—180 Days of Problem Solving

Name: _____

 **DIRECTIONS:** Trace the shapes. Then, draw lines to connect the matching shapes.

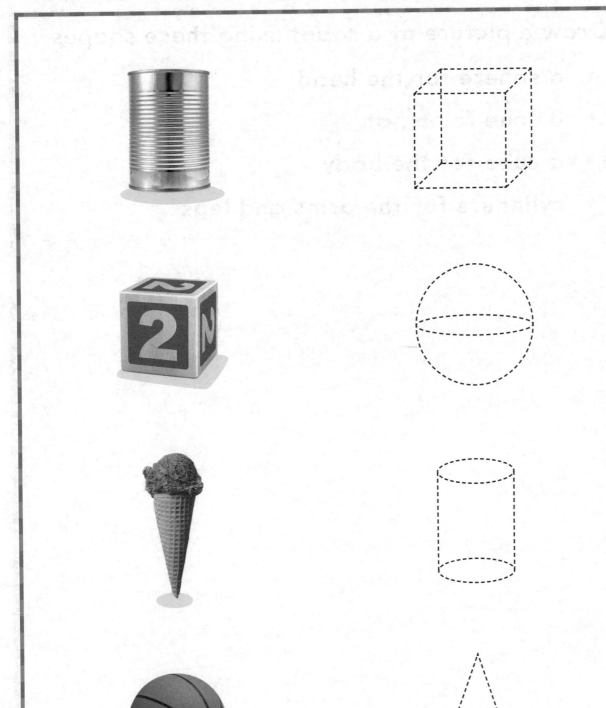

Challenge Yourself!

Name: ______________________________

DIRECTIONS: Read the problem. Solve the problem.

Draw a picture of a robot using these shapes:

- a sphere for the head
- a cone for a hat
- a cube for the body
- cylinders for the arms and legs

Name: _____

DIRECTIONS: Think about the problem.

Maya says a cone and a cylinder have circle faces. Is she correct?

Circle the cones and cylinders. Draw an X on the shapes that are not cones or cylinders.

Name: _____

DIRECTIONS: Read the problem. Solve the problem. Circle your answer.

Problem: Adam says his cereal box is a cube. Do you agree with him?

What Do You Know?

_____

A cube has _____ faces.

Each face of a cube is a _____.

What Is Your Plan?

Compare the shape to a cube.

_____

This shape has _____ faces.

Each face of this shape is a _____.

Solve the Problem!

Yes   No

Picture It!

Name: _____

 DIRECTIONS: Look at the example. Solve the problem.

Example: Circle the shape that has more circle faces.

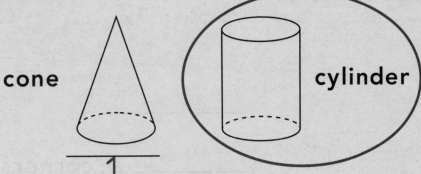

cone

cylinder

A cone has _____1_____ circle face.

A cylinder has _____2_____ circle faces.

Circle the shape that has more faces.

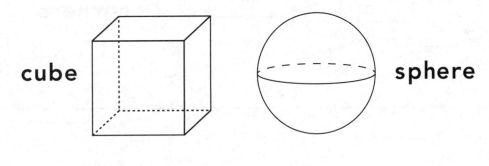

cube

sphere

A cube has _____ faces.

A sphere has _____ faces.

Draw It!

Name: _____

DIRECTIONS:
Trace the pictures to solve the problem.

How many corners do these shapes have?
Circle the corners.

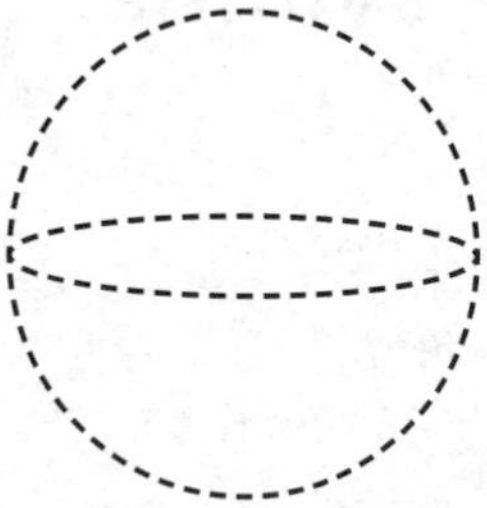

_____
- - - - - - -
_____ corners

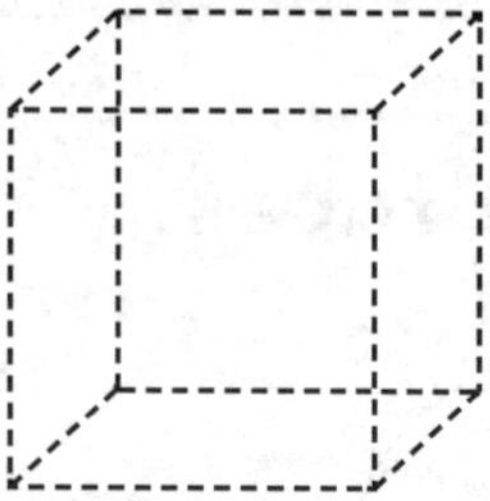

_____
- - - - - - -
_____ corners

_____
- - - - - - -
_____ corners

#51612—180 Days of Problem Solving

Name: _____

DIRECTIONS: Read the problem. Solve the problem. Write your answers.

1. How are these shapes the same?

 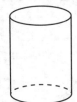

A cone and a cylinder both have

_____

- - - - - - - - - - -

_____ faces.

2. How are both of these shapes the same?

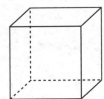 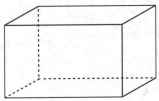

_____
- - - -

Both of these shapes have _____ corners.

3. How are these shapes different?

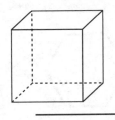 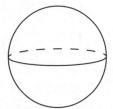

_____
- - - -

A cube has _____ faces.

_____
- - - -

A sphere has _____ faces.

Think About It!

Name: _____

DIRECTIONS: Think about the problem.

Adam is sorting objects. He puts all the flat objects in a group. He puts all the solid objects in a group. Which group has more?

Circle all the flat shapes. Draw an X on the solid shapes.

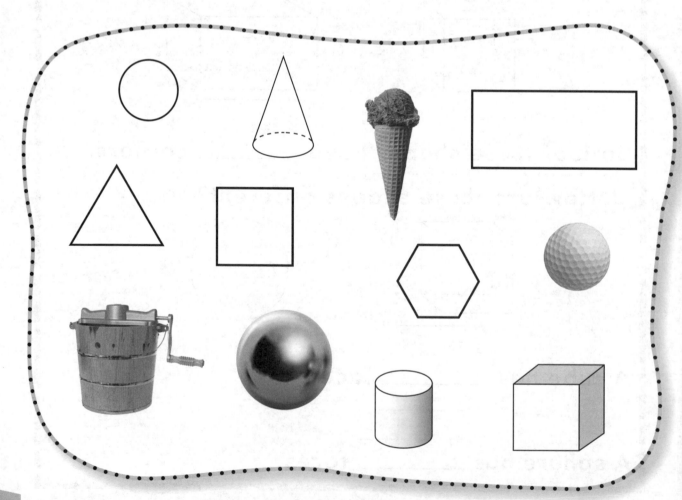

Name: _____

 DIRECTIONS: Read the problem. Solve the problem. Circle your answer.

Problem: Emma has 6 shapes. She puts the flat shapes in a group. She puts the solid shapes in a group. Which group has fewer shapes?

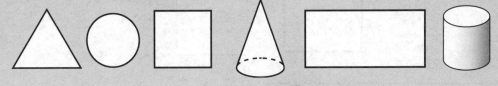

? What Do You Know?

Draw the flat shapes.

Draw the solid shapes.

🔑 What Is Your Plan?

Count the shapes in each group.

_____
_ _ _ _ _
_____ flat shapes

_____
_ _ _ _ _
_____ solid shapes

💡 Solve the Problem!

flat shapes   solid shapes

Picture It!

Name: _____

DIRECTIONS: Look at the example. Solve the problem.

Example: How are these shapes different?

A _____square_____ is flat.

A _____cube_____ is solid.

How are these shapes different?

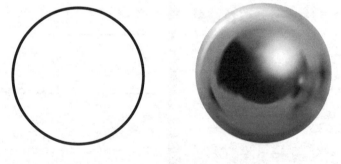

A _____ is flat.

A _____ is solid.

Name: _____

 **DIRECTIONS:** Draw a picture to show the problem.

What shape is the face of each solid shape?
Draw the shape.

Solid Shape	Flat Shape

Name: _____

DIRECTIONS: Read the problem. Solve the problem.

What is your favorite place to go with your family? Draw a picture of the place with these shapes:

- 4 squares
- 3 circles
- 1 cube
- 2 triangles

- 1 cone
- 3 rectangles
- 1 cylinder
- 2 spheres

ANSWER KEY

Week 1: Day 1 (page 13)
Student should have drawn 2 boys and a basket with 3 apples.

Week 1: Day 2 (page 14)
No; Student should have drawn 3 girls and 2 balls. Student should have also counted to find how many girls and how many balls.

Week 1: Day 3 (page 15)
1. 3; Student should have drawn lines to connect the cats to their corresponding numbers and circled 3.
2. 5; Student should have drawn lines to connect the dogs to their corresponding numbers and circled 5.

Week 1: Day 4 (page 16)
Yes; Student should have drawn 3 dogs and 3 leashes. Student should have also drawn lines to connect the dogs and leashes to their corresponding numbers.

Week 1: Day 5 (page 17)
3 cups of tea

Week 2: Day 1 (page 18)
Student should have drawn a picture of 7 bears with each bear wearing a hat.

Week 2: Day 2 (page 19)
9; Student should have circled 9 flowers and drawn one leaf on each flower.

Week 2: Day 3 (page 20)
10; Student should have drawn lines to connect each cup and straw to its corresponding number.

Week 2: Day 4 (page 21)
8; Student should have drawn a picture of 8 boys with each boy having one baseball.

Week 2: Day 5 (page 22)
Yes

Week 3: Day 1 (page 23)
Group 2

Week 3: Day 2 (page 24)
Box 1 and Box 2 both have 7 suns; Each box has suns. Student should have counted the suns in each box.

Week 3: Day 3 (page 25)
Sally's rings: 6; Rosa's rings: 8

Week 3: Day 4 (page 26)
Yes; Student should have drawn 5 happy faces in Box 2 and circled 5 for both boxes.

Week 3: Day 5 (page 27)
No; Student should have drawn dots in Box 2 that represent his or her age.

Week 4: Day 1 (page 28)
Student may count on from 3 or count each coin.

Week 4: Day 2 (page 29)
9; 2 marbles are in the bag; Student should have counted on from 2.

Week 4: Day 3 (page 30)
7; Student should have counted on from 3.

Week 4: Day 4 (page 31)
6; Student should have drawn 3 more bugs and counted on from 3.

Week 4: Day 5 (page 32)
5; Student should have drawn 10 seashells. Student may have drawn a circle around the first 5 seashells and counted on from 5.

Week 5: Day 1 (page 33)
Student should have drawn 8 flowers.

Week 5: Day 2 (page 34)
5; Student should have drawn 5 blocks and counted them.

Week 5: Day 3 (page 35)
4; Student should have circled the 3 fish, drawn a line connecting the 3 fish to the number 3 and an arrow from 3 to 4, and circled 4.

Week 5: Day 4 (page 36)
6; Student should have drawn 6 pets and circled 6.

Week 5: Day 5 (page 37)
Ted: 4; Luis: 5; Dante: 6; Student should have circled the corresponding numbers for each airplane.

Week 6: Day 1 (page 38)
Student should have drawn 3 strawberries on the plate.

ANSWER KEY *(cont.)*

Week 6: Day 2 (page 39)

2; Student should have traced the words "dog" and "spots." Student should have also counted 2 spots and traced the numbers 1 and 2.

Week 6: Day 3 (page 40)

5; Student should have drawn a hat for each boy. Student should have also counted the hats and traced the numbers 1–5

Week 6: Day 4 (page 41)

Student should have drawn 4 bells on the collar. Student should have also counted and traced numbers 1–4.

Week 6: Day 5 (page 42)

1. 3; Student should have counted the 3 boys wearing caps and traced the numbers 1–3.
2. 2; Student should have counted the 2 boys not wearing caps and traced the numbers 1 and 2.

Week 7: Day 1 (page 43)

Student should have drawn 6 candles.

Week 7: Day 2 (page 44)

9; Student should have traced the word "fish." Student should have also counted and written the numbers 1–9.

Week 7: Day 3 (page 45)

6; Student should have drawn a bird in each nest. Student should have also counted the birds and traced the numbers 1–6.

Week 7: Day 4 (page 46)

8; Student should have drawn a flower in each vase. Student should have also counted and traced the numbers 1–8.

Week 7: Day 5 (page 47)

7; Student should have counted the lizards and traced the numbers 1–7.

Week 8: Day 1 (page 48)

Student should have drawn 19 clouds.

Week 8: Day 2 (page 49)

13; Student should have traced the word "birds." Student should have also counted the birds and written the numbers 1–13.

Week 8: Day 3 (page 50)

11; Student should have drawn one acorn for each squirrel. Student should have also counted the acorns.

Week 8: Day 4 (page 51)

16; Student should have counted the plates and traced the numbers 1–16.

Week 8: Day 5 (page 52)

15; Student should have counted the stripes and traced the numbers 1–15.

Week 9: Day 1 (page 53)

Student should have completed the picture by drawing 10 pencils in each of the 3 boxes.

Week 9: Day 2 (page 54)

40; Student should have drawn 10 granola bars in each box. Student should have also counted by tens and circled 10, 20, 30, and 40.

Week 9: Day 3 (page 55)

50; Student should have drawn lines from each hive to its corresponding multiple of ten. Student should have also counted by tens and circled 50.

Week 9: Day 4 (page 56)

60; Student should have drawn 10 oranges in each box and circled 60.

Week 9: Day 5 (page 57)

9; Student should have drawn groups of 10 beads in 9 bags for a total of 90 beads.

Week 10: Day 1 (page 58)

Yes; Student may have counted each set of butterflies to show each set has 5 and is equal, or student may have drawn lines matching each butterfly in one set to a corresponding butterfly in the other set to show each set is equal.

Week 10: Day 2 (page 59)

No; Ali's necklace has 6 beads. Ella's necklace has 9 beads. Student should have counted the beads in each necklace, or student may have drawn lines to match each bead in one set to a corresponding bead in the other set to show the sets are not equal.

Week 10: Day 3 (page 60)

No; Student should have drawn lines to match the objects to show the sets are not equal.

ANSWER KEY *(cont.)*

Week 10: Day 4 (page 61)

Yes; Student should have drawn a picture to show how to compare the number of cherries in each group. Student may have drawn 9 cherries in both groups and drawn lines to match each cherry in one set to a corresponding cherry in the other set to show the sets are equal.

Week 10: Day 5 (page 62)

6; Student should have drawn a picture to show 6 baseballs in each box. Student should have also moved 1 baseball from the box with 7 baseballs to the box with 5 baseballs.

Week 11: Day 1 (page 63)

Student should have circled the jellyfish. Student may have drawn lines to match each jellyfish to a corresponding seahorse to show that there are more jellyfish.

Week 11: Day 2 (page 64)

coconuts; Student should have counted 4 palm trees and 7 coconuts and written the numbers. Student may have compared the numbers by drawing lines to match each palm tree to a corresponding coconut to show the group of coconuts is greater.

Week 11: Day 3 (page 65)

5 is greater than 4; Student should have drawn lines to match each fish to a corresponding crab and drawn a circle around the group of fish to show the group is greater.

Week 11: Day 4 (page 66)

Rick; Student should have counted 2 apples for Ken and 4 apples for Rick.

Week 11: Day 5 (page 67)

1. Student should have written any number greater than 3.
2. Student should have written the number 9.
3. Student should have written any number greater than 5.
4. Student should have written the number 7.

Week 12: Day 1 (page 68)

Student should have circled the tomatoes. Student may have drawn lines to match each carrot to a corresponding tomato to show there are fewer tomatoes.

Week 12: Day 2 (page 69)

crackers; Student should have counted 7 crackers and 10 cookies and written the numbers. Student may have compared the number of crackers and cookies by drawing lines to match each cracker to a corresponding cookie to show there are fewer crackers.

Week 12: Day 3 (page 70)

frogs; Student should have drawn lines to match each frog to a corresponding mouse and drawn a circle around the group of frogs to show the group is less.

Week 12: Day 4 (page 71)

Otis; Student should have drawn 8 coins for Otis and 9 coins for Jan. Student may have drawn lines to match each of Otis's coins to each of Jan's coins to show Otis has fewer coins.

Week 12: Day 5 (page 72)

1. Student should have written any number less than 6.
2. Student should have written the number 5.
3. Student should have written any number greater than 2.
4. Student should have written the number 10.

Week 13: Day 1 (page 73)

Student should have drawn 2 animal stickers and 4 plant stickers. Student may have drawn lines to match each animal sticker to a corresponding plant sticker to show the group with plant stickers is greater.

Week 13: Day 2 (page 74)

5 is greater than 3; Student should have drawn 5 red marbles and 3 blue marbles. Student may have compared the marbles by drawing lines to match each red marble to a corresponding blue marble to show the group of red marbles is greater.

Week 13: Day 3 (page 75)

2 is less than 3; Student should have drawn lines to match each of Sal's buttons to a corresponding button on Pam's shirt to show Sal's shirt has fewer buttons.

ANSWER KEY *(cont.)*

Week 13: Day 4 (page 76)

Min; Student should have drawn a picture to show Pedro has 4 grapes and Min has 2 grapes. Student may have drawn lines to match each of Pedro's grapes to a corresponding grape in Min's group.

Week 13: Day 5 (page 77)

Student should have drawn a picture to show Pia has 3 cats, Saul has 1 cat, and Leo has 4 cats. Leo has the most cats. Saul has the fewest cats.

Week 14: Day 1 (page 78)

Student should have drawn 7 green marbles and 10 yellow marbles. Student may have drawn lines to match each green marble to a corresponding yellow marble to show the group of yellow marbles is greater.

Week 14: Day 2 (page 79)

Tia; Student should have drawn 8 blocks for Tia and 5 blocks for Andy. Student may have compared the numbers by drawing 8 blocks and 5 blocks and lines to match them to show the group of 8 is greater.

Week 14: Day 3 (page 80)

4 is less than 6. Student should have drawn 4 bugs on the first leaf and 6 bugs on the second leaf and lines to match each bug on the first leaf to a corresponding bug on the second leaf.

Week 14: Day 4 (page 81)

5 is less than 7; Student should have drawn a picture to show Jim has 5 hats and Pat has 7 hats. Student may have drawn lines to match each of Jim's hats to a corresponding hat for Pat.

Week 14: Day 5 (page 82)

1. Possible answer: 4 is greater than 3.
2. Possible answer: 2 is less than 5.
3. Possible answer: 10 is more than 6.
4. Possible answer: 1 is less than 7.

Week 15: Day 1 (page 83)

Student should have drawn 8 big buttons in the first circle and 7 small buttons in the second circle

Week 15: Day 2 (page 84)

There are 7 trucks in Lot A. There are 6 trucks in Lot B. The big trucks park in Lot A. The small trucks park in Lot B. Student may have sorted the trucks by drawing 7 big trucks in one group and 6 small trucks in another group.

Week 15: Day 3 (page 85)

Big cars; 4 big cars; 3 small cars; Student should have drawn an arrow to each car to show which are big and which are small.

Week 15: Day 4 (page 86)

Student should have drawn 2 small eggs in the basket labeled "small eggs" and written the number 2. Student should have drawn 5 eggs in the basket labeled "medium eggs" and written the number 5. Student should have drawn 3 large eggs in the basket labeled "large eggs" and written the number 3.

Week 15: Day 5 (page 87)

1. 4
2. Student should have made 4 groups with 4 tiny leaves in one group, 2 small leaves in a second group, 3 medium leaves in a third group, and 1 large leaf in a fourth group.
3. Student should have circled the group with 1 large leaf to show it has the fewest leaves.
4. Student should have put an X on the group with 4 tiny leaves to show it has the most leaves.

Week 16: Day 1 (page 88)

Student should have drawn 10 blue marbles in one bag and 6 orange marbles in the other bag.

Week 16: Day 2 (page 89)

There are fewer green apples. 6 red apples; 4 green apples; Student should have sorted the apples by drawing 6 red apples in one bag and 4 green apples in the other bag.

Week 16: Day 3 (page 90)

White blocks; gray: 4; white: 9; Student should have counted 4 gray blocks and 9 white blocks.

Week 16: Day 4 (page 91)

7 black rings; 4 white rings; 5 gray rings; Student should have drawn 7 black rings in the first jewelry box, 4 white rings in the second jewelry box, and 5 gray rings in the third jewelry box.

ANSWER KEY *(cont.)*

Week 16: Day 5 (page 92)
1. 4
2. Student should have made 4 groups with 4 gray dresses in one group, 3 white dresses in a second group, 2 black dresses in a third group, and 1 black dress with white polka dots in a fourth group.
3. Student should have circled the group with 1 black dress with white polka dots to show it has the fewest dresses.
4. Student should have put an X on the group with 4 gray dresses to show it has the most dresses.

Week 17: Day 1 (page 93)
Student may have sorted the buttons by color by drawing the white buttons in one group and the black buttons in the other group. Student may have sorted the buttons by size by drawing the small buttons in one group and the large buttons in the other group. Student may have also sorted the buttons by shape by drawing the round buttons in one group and the square buttons in the other group

Week 17: Day 2 (page 94)
There are 4 flowers in one group. There are 4 flowers in the other group. A flower shop sorts flowers. The flowers are sorted into 2 groups. Student should have sorted the flowers by making two groups. Student may have sorted the flowers by size by drawing the large flowers in one group and the small flowers in the other group.

Week 17: Day 3 (page 95)
Student should have sorted the fish by color (3 white fish and 3 gray fish) and by spots (4 fish have spots, 2 fish do not have spots).

Week 17: Day 4 (page 96)
There are 3 shirts in one group. There are 3 shirts in the other group. Student may have sorted the shirts by size (3 small shirts and 3 big shirts). Student may have also sorted the shirts by color (3 gray shirts and 3 white shirts).

Week 17: Day 5 (page 97)
1. Student should have colored the hearts using 3 different colors. Student may have sorted the hearts by size by drawing 2 large hearts in one group, 2 medium hearts in a second group, and 2 small hearts in a third group.
2. Student may have sorted the hearts by color by drawing the hearts colored in one color in one group, the hearts colored in a second color in a second group, and the hearts colored in a third color in a third group.

Week 18: Day 1 (page 98)
Student should have drawn a tall tree, a long bench, and a short flower.

Week 18: Day 2 (page 99)
The crayon is light. The book is heavy. Allen has a crayon. Allen has a book. Student should have described the crayon as light and the book as heavy.

Week 18: Day 3 (page 100)
1. Long; heavy
2. Short; light

Week 18: Day 4 (page 101)
Student should have drawn a long snake, a short bird, and a heavy dog.

Week 18: Day 5 (page 102)
1. Possible answer: pencil; feather; stick
2. Possible answer: rock; big book; brick
3. Possible answer: airplane; truck; boat
4. Possible answer: seashell; penny; eraser

Week 19: Day 1 (page 103)
Student should have drawn a building that looks taller than a house, a worm that looks shorter than a snake, and a car that looks heavier than a bike.

Week 19: Day 2 (page 104)
Pencil; Kimi has a pencil. Her friend has a crayon. Student should have compared the lengths of the objects by saying the pencil is longer.

Week 19: Day 3 (page 105)
A rock is heavier than a strawberry.

ANSWER KEY *(cont.)*

Week 19: Day 4 (page 106)

Student should have drawn the monkey first to show it is the shortest, the lion second to show it is in the middle, and the giraffe third to show it is the tallest.

Week 19: Day 5 (page 107)

1. Possible answer: pencil and crayon with the crayon drawn longer
2. Possible answer: car and cat
3. Possible answer: flower and tree with the flower drawn shorter
4. Possible answer: feather and basketball

Week 20: Day 1 (page 108)

Student should have drawn a total of 4 ducks swimming in the pond.

Week 20: Day 2 (page 109)

4; There are 3 cows. There is 1 horse. Student should have drawn 3 cows and 1 horse and counted the animals to find the total.

Week 20: Day 3 (page 110)

3; Student should have drawn 2 more goldfish in the bowl for a total of 3 goldfish.

Week 20: Day 4 (page 111)

5; Student should have drawn 2 red flowers and 3 yellow flowers in the vase.

Week 20: Day 5 (page 112)

2; Student should have drawn 2 green dresses and 2 red dresses to show Kiki has a total of 4 dresses.

Week 21: Day 1 (page 113)

Student should have drawn 4 more birds on the branch for a total of 7 birds.

Week 21: Day 2 (page 114)

9; Student should have drawn a total of 9 bunnies. Student should have counted the bunnies and written the numbers 1–9.

Week 21: Day 3 (page 115)

6; Student should have drawn 1 more kitten for a total of 6 kittens.

Week 21: Day 4 (page 116)

10; Student should have drawn 7 brown eggs and 3 white eggs for a total of 10 eggs.

Week 21: Day 5 (page 117)

2; Student should have drawn 6 yellow flowers and 2 pink flowers to show a total of 8 flowers.

Week 22: Day 1 (page 118)

Student should have drawn 4 puppies for a total of 6 puppies.

Week 22: Day 2 (page 119)

9; Student should have drawn 1 red bug and 8 green bugs. Student should have written the number sentence 1 + 8 = 9.

Week 22: Day 3 (page 120)

7; Student should have drawn 4 blue pens and 3 red pens. 4 + 3 = 7

Week 22: Day 4 (page 121)

4; 6 + 4 = 10; Student should have drawn 6 red bows and 4 pink bows to show a total of 10 bows.

Week 22: Day 5 (page 122)

5 red; 2 + 1 + 5 = 8; Student should have drawn 2 green frogs, 1 orange frog, and 5 red frogs for a total of 8 frogs.

Week 23: Day 1 (page 123)

Student should have colored a combination of 5 red and green apples. Possible combinations: 1 red and 4 green; 2 red and 3 green; 3 red and 2 green; 4 red and 1 green

Week 23: Day 2 (page 124)

2 blue crayons and 1 black crayon; 1 blue crayon and 2 black crayons; There are 3 crayons in the box. There are blue crayons. There are black crayons. Student should have drawn the crayons two different ways.

Week 23: Day 3 (page 125)

Student should have drawn 2 dots in one part and 2 dots in the other part and written the number sentence 2 + 2 = 4. Student should have also drawn 3 dots in one part and 1 dot in the other part and written the number sentence 3 + 1 = 4 or 1 + 3 = 4.

Week 23: Day 4 (page 126)

Student should have drawn 4 combinations of 8 red and yellow happy face stickers. Possible combinations: 1 red and 7 yellow; 2 red and 6 yellow; 3 red and 5 yellow; 4 red and 4 yellow; 5 red and 3 yellow; 6 red and 2 yellow; 7 red and 1 yellow

ANSWER KEY *(cont.)*

Week 23: Day 5 (page 127)

Student should have drawn six combinations of 7 purple and green grapes. Possible combinations: 1 purple and 6 green; 2 purple and 5 green; 3 purple and 4 green; 4 purple and 3 green; 5 purple and 2 green; 6 purple and 1 green

Week 24: Day 1 (page 128)

Student should have drawn 6 more crayons to show a total of 10 crayons in the box.

Week 24: Day 2 (page 129)

3; A full box has 10 markers. Jay has 7 markers. Student should have drawn 3 more markers to show a total of 10 markers in the box.

Week 24: Day 3 (page 130)

4; Student should have colored in 6 circles in the ten frame and written the numbers 1–4 in the remaining circles.

Week 24: Day 4 (page 131)

2; Student should have shaded in 8 circles and may have written the numbers 1 and 2 in the remaining circles.

Week 24: Day 5 (page 132)

6 blue pens; 4 green pens; Student should have drawn 6 blue pens and 4 green pens to show there are 2 more blue pens than green pens.

Week 25: Day 1 (page 133)

Student should have drawn a picture of 2 birds in the nest and may have drawn 1 bird flying away.

Week 25: Day 2 (page 134)

2; Student may have drawn 4 babies on the rug and crossed out 2 of the babies. Student should have written the number sentence 4 − 2 = 2.

Week 25: Day 3 (page 135)

2; 3 − 1 = 2; Student should have crossed out 1 peach.

Week 25: Day 4 (page 136)

2; Student should have drawn 5 toy cars and crossed out 3 toy cars.

Week 25: Day 5 (page 137)

1; Student should have drawn 4 slices of pizza and crossed out 3 slices.

Week 26: Day 1 (page 138)

Student may have drawn 5 cars in the parking lot and may have drawn 4 cars driving away.

Week 26: Day 2 (page 139)

3; Student should have drawn 8 boats and crossed out 5. Student should have written the number sentence 8 − 5 = 3.

Week 26: Day 3 (page 140)

2; 7 − 5 = 2; Student should have crossed out 5 of the 7 dogs.

Week 26: Day 4 (page 141)

4; Student should have drawn 10 hot air balloons and crossed out 6 of them, or student may have drawn a group of 4 hot air balloons and 6 hot air balloons flying away.

Week 26: Day 5 (page 142)

3; Student should have drawn a picture with 3 red balloons, 3 yellow balloons, and 3 blue balloons to show a total of 9 balloons.

Week 27: Day 1 (page 143)

Student should have drawn 4 sheep in the barn and 2 sheep outside of the barn.

Week 27: Day 2 (page 144)

5; Student should have drawn 10 cows and crossed out 5 of them. Student should have written the number sentence 10 − 5 = 5.

Week 27: Day 3 (page 145)

4; 7 − 3 = 4; Student should have crossed out 3 of the 7 ducks.

Week 27: Day 4 (page 146)

6; 8 − 2 = 6; Student should have drawn 8 butterflies and crossed out 2 butterflies, or student may have drawn 6 butterflies on the bush and 2 butterflies flying away.

Week 27: Day 5 (page 147)

1. Student should have drawn 2 hens in the yard, 3 hens in the coop, and 5 hens in the barn.
2. 10 − 2 − 3 = 5
3. 5

Week 28: Day 1 (page 148)

Student should have colored 12 circles in the ten frames.

Week 28: Day 2 (page 149)

16; Phil has hats for his birthday party. Student should have colored 16 circles in the ten frames. Student may have counted on from 10 to find how many hats.

ANSWER KEY *(cont.)*

Week 28: Day 3 (page 150)

15; 10 + 5 = 15; Student should have labeled 15 circles in the ten frames.

Week 28: Day 4 (page 151)

17; 10 + 7 = 17; Student should have colored or labeled 17 circles in the ten frames.

Week 28: Day 5 (page 152)

1. Student should have colored or labeled 19 circles in the ten frames.
2. 10 + 2 + 7 = 19
3. 19

Week 29: Day 1 (page 153)

Student should have drawn 10 dots in the circle.

Week 29: Day 2 (page 154)

3; Student should have drawn 10 dots in the "10" circle. Student should have drawn 3 dots in the other circle. Student should have written the number sentence 10 + 3 = 13.

Week 29: Day 3 (page 155)

4; 10 + 4 = 14; Student should have labeled the circles outside the bag with 11–14.

Week 29: Day 4 (page 156)

4; 10 + 4 = 14; Student should have drawn 4 circles outside the ten frame; student may have labeled the circles inside the frame with 1–10 and the circles outside the frame with 11–14.

Week 29: Day 5 (page 157)

1. Student should have drawn a picture of 10 pancakes on the first plate, 3 pancakes on the second plate, and 5 pancakes on the last plate.
2. 10 + 3 + 5 = 18
3. 5

Week 30: Day 1 (page 158)

Student should have circled the 3 rectangles.

Week 30: Day 2 (page 159)

Yes; A square has 4 equal sides. A square has 4 corners. Student should have compared Kelly's sandwich to what he or she knows about squares by saying the sandwich has 4 equal sides and 4 corners.

Week 30: Day 3 (page 160)

3; 3; yes

Week 30: Day 4 (page 161)

Shape	Sides	Angles
▢	4	4
△	3	3
○	0	0
⬡	6	6

Week 30: Day 5 (page 162)

Student should have drawn a pig using a circle for the head, 2 small triangles for the ears, a rectangle for the body, four small squares for the feet, a small hexagon for the nose, and two small circles for the eyes.

Week 31: Day 1 (page 163)

Student should have circled the 2 squares and the 2 rectangles and put an X on all the remaining shapes.

Week 31: Day 2 (page 164)

No; A triangle has 3 sides. A triangle has 3 angles. This shape has 3 sides. This shape has 0 angles. No

Week 31: Day 3 (page 165)

A rectangle has more sides than a triangle. Student should have labeled the sides of the rectangle with 1–4 and the triangle with 1–3.

Week 31: Day 4 (page 166)

Possible triangles: 3 equal sides, 2 equal sides, 0 equal sides; right triangle; Student should have drawn a square and a rectangle.

Week 31: Day 5 (page 167)

Student should have drawn a picture with 2 circles, 2 triangles, 4 rectangles, and 1 square.

ANSWER KEY *(cont.)*

Week 32: Day 1 (page 168)

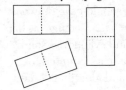

Week 32: Day 2 (page 169)

Yes; A triangle has 3 sides. A triangle has 3 angles. A square has 4 equal sides. A square has 4 corners. Student should have drawn a square and a diagonal line to show the square partitioned into 2 right triangles.

Week 32: Day 3 (page 170)

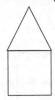

Week 32: Day 4 (page 171)

1. 3 triangles
2. 4 triangles
3. 6 triangles

Week 32: Day 5 (page 172)

1. Student may have drawn a square using triangles.
2. Student may have drawn a rectangle using triangles.
3. Student may have drawn a trapezoid using triangles.

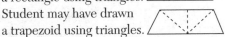

Week 33: Day 1 (page 173)

Student may have drawn a house using a square and a triangle, and a tree using a rectangle and a square.

Week 33: Day 2 (page 174)

Student drawing should show 4 triangles, 3 rectangles, and 2 squares. Student should have drawn a triangle, rectangle, and square. Student should have written he or she needs to draw 4 triangles, 3 rectangles, and 2 squares.

Week 33: Day 3 (page 175)

Yes; no; yes; no

Week 33: Day 4 (page 176)

Student should have drawn a picture with a square next to a rectangle, a triangle below the rectangle, a circle above the rectangle, and a rectangle beside the triangle. Possible drawing:

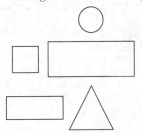

Week 33: Day 5 (page 177)

Student should have drawn a picture with 1 circle, 1 rectangle, and 1 triangle. Possible sentences: My rectangle is beside my circle. My circle is above my triangle. My triangle is below my circle. Possible drawing:

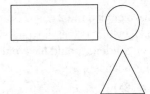

Week 34: Day 1 (page 178)

Student should have circled the 3 spheres (orange, Earth, ball of yarn).

Week 34: Day 2 (page 179)

Yes; Student should have drawn a cone. Student may have compared Joe's hat to the drawing by saying both have a circle face and a point at the top.

Week 34: Day 3 (page 180)

Student should have drawn a square and written the word "square."

ANSWER KEY *(cont.)*

Week 34: Day 4 (page 181)

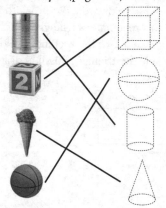

Week 34: Day 5 (page 182)

Student should have drawn a picture of a robot using a sphere for the head, a cone for the hat, a cube for the body, and cylinders for the arms and legs.

Week 35: Day 1 (page 183)

Student should have circled the 2 cones (safety cone, teepee) and 3 cylinders (candle, paper towel roll, battery). Student should have put an X on the remaining shapes.

Week 35: Day 2 (page 184)

No; A cube has 6 faces. Each face of a cube is a square. This shape has 6 faces. Each face of this shape is a rectangle.

Week 35: Day 3 (page 185)

A cube has 6 faces. A sphere has 0 faces. Student should have circled the cube.

Week 35: Day 4 (page 186)

A sphere has 0 corners. A cube has 8 corners. A cylinder has 0 corners.

Week 35: Day 5 (page 187)

1. Circle
2. 8
3. A cube has all 6 faces. A sphere has 0 faces.

Week 36: Day 1 (page 188)

Student should have circled the flat, 2-dimensional shapes (circle, square, triangle, rectangle, and hexagon). Student should have put an X on the solid, 3-dimensional shapes (cube, sphere, cylinder, cone).

Week 36: Day 2 (page 189)

Solid shapes; Student should have drawn a triangle, circle, square, and rectangle as flat shapes and the cone and cylinder as solid shapes. Student should have counted the shapes in each group and identified 4 flat shapes and 2 solid shapes.

Week 36: Day 3 (page 190)

A circle is flat. A sphere is solid.

Week 36: Day 4 (page 191)

Solid shape	Flat shape
(cone)	(circle)
(cube)	(square)
(cylinder)	(circle)

Week 36: Day 5 (page 192)

Student should have drawn a picture of their favorite place to go with his or her family using these shapes: 4 squares, 3 circles, 1 cube, 2 triangles, 1 cone, 3 rectangles, 1 cylinder, and 2 spheres.

PRACTICE PAGE RUBRIC

Directions: Evaluate student work in each category by choosing one number in each row. Students have opportunities to score up to four points in each row and up to 16 points total.

	Advanced	Proficient	Developing	Beginning
Problem-solving strategies	Uses multiple efficient strategies Uses a detailed and appropriate visual model	Uses appropriate strategies Uses an appropriate visual model	Demonstrates some form of strategic approach Uses a visual model but is incomplete	No strategic approach is evident No visual model is attempted
Points	4	3	2	1
Mathematical knowledge	Provides correct solutions and multiple solutions when relevant Connects and applies the concept in complex ways	Provides correct solutions Demonstrates proficiency of concept	Shows some correct solutions Demonstrates some proficiency of concept	No solutions are correct Does not demonstrate proficiency of concept
Points	4	3	2	1
Explanation	Explains and justifies thinking thoroughly and clearly	Explains and justifies thinking	Explains thinking but difficult to follow	Offers no explanation of thinking
Points	4	3	2	1
Organization	Well-planned, well-organized, and complete	Shows a plan and is complete	Shows some planning and is mostly complete	Shows no planning and is mostly incomplete
Points	4	3	2	1

PRACTICE PAGE ITEM ANALYSIS

Directions: Record students' rubric scores (page 203) for the Day 5 practice page in the appropriate columns. Add the totals and record the sums in the Total Scores column. You can view: (1) which students are not understanding the mathematical concepts and problem-solving steps, and (2) how students progress after multiple encounters with the problem-solving process.

Student Name	Week 1	Week 2	Week 3	Week 4	Week 5	Week 6	Week 7	Week 8	Week 9	Total Scores
Average Class Score										

PRACTICE PAGE ITEM ANALYSIS *(cont.)*

Directions: Record students' rubric scores (page 203) for the Day 5 practice page in the appropriate columns. Add the totals and record the sums in the Total Scores column. You can view: (1) which students are not understanding the mathematical concepts and problem-solving steps, and (2) how students progress after multiple encounters with the problem-solving process.

Student Name	Week 10	Week 11	Week 12	Week 13	Week 14	Week 15	Week 16	Week 17	Week 18	Total Scores
Average Class Score										

PRACTICE PAGE ITEM ANALYSIS (cont.)

Directions: Record students' rubric scores (page 203) for the Day 5 practice page in the appropriate columns. Add the totals and record the sums in the Total Scores column. You can view: (1) which students are not understanding the mathematical concepts and problem-solving steps, and (2) how students progress after multiple encounters with the problem-solving process.

Student Name	Week 19	Week 20	Week 21	Week 22	Week 23	Week 24	Week 25	Week 26	Week 27	Total Scores
Average Class Score										

PRACTICE PAGE ITEM ANALYSIS *(cont.)*

Directions: Record students' rubric scores (page 203) for the Day 5 practice page in the appropriate columns. Add the totals and record the sums in the Total Scores column. You can view: (1) which students are not understanding the mathematical concepts and problem-solving steps, and (2) how students progress after multiple encounters with the problem-solving process.

Student Name	Week 28	Week 29	Week 30	Week 31	Week 32	Week 33	Week 34	Week 35	Week 36	Total Scores
Average Class Score										

STUDENT ITEM ANALYSIS

Directions: Record individual student's rubric scores (page 203) for each practice page in the appropriate columns. Add the totals and record the sums in the Total Scores column. You can view: (1) which concepts and problem-solving steps the student is not understanding and (2) how the student is progressing after multiple encounters with the problem-solving process.

Student Name:	Day 1	Day 2	Day 3	Day 4	Day 5	Total Scores
Week 1						
Week 2						
Week 3						
Week 4						
Week 5						
Week 6						
Week 7						
Week 8						
Week 9						
Week 10						
Week 11						
Week 12						
Week 13						
Week 14						
Week 15						
Week 16						
Week 17						
Week 18						
Week 19						
Week 20						
Week 21						
Week 22						
Week 23						
Week 24						
Week 25						
Week 26						
Week 27						
Week 28						
Week 29						
Week 30						
Week 31						
Week 32						
Week 33						
Week 34						
Week 35						
Week 36						

PROBLEM-SOLVING FRAMEWORK

Use the following problem-solving steps to help you:

1. understand the problem
2. make a plan
3. solve the problem
4. check your answer and explain your thinking

What Do You Know?

- read the problem
- say the problem in your own words
- picture the problem
- find the important information
- understand the question

What Is Your Plan?

- draw a picture or model
- choose a strategy
- choose an operation (+, −)
- decide how many steps there are

Solve the Problem!

- carry out your plan
- check your steps
- decide if your strategy works or choose a new strategy
- find the answer

Look Back and Explain!

- check your answer to see if it makes sense
- decide if there are other possible answers
- use words to explain your answer

PROBLEM-SOLVING STRATEGIES

Draw a picture.	Make a table or list.	Use a number sentence.
🧁 + 🧁 = 🧁🧁		$10 + 4 = 14$

Make a model.	Look for a pattern.	Act it out.
Whole: 19 — Part: 10 — Part: 9	 3, 6, 9, 12, 15, __18__	

Solve a simpler problem.	Work backward.	Use logical reasoning.
7 + 6 7 + 3 + 3 10 + 3 = 13	⟵ ? + 3 + 5 = 18	

Guess and check.	Create a graph.	Use concrete objects.
2 + ☐ + 5 = 11 2 + 4 + 5 = 11 11 = 11 Yes!	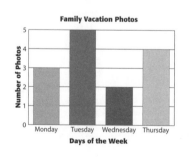	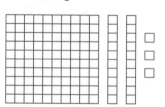 base-ten blocks

   #51612—180 Days of Problem Solving

DIGITAL RESOURCES

Teacher Resources

Resource	Filename
Practice Page Rubric	rubric.pdf
Practice Page Item Analysis	itemanalysis.pdf itemanalysis.docx itemanalysis.xlsx
Student Item Analysis	studentitem.pdf studentitem.docx studentitem.xlsx

Student Resources

Resource	Filename
Problem-Solving Framework	framework.pdf
Problem-Solving Strategies	strategies.pdf

NOTES

NOTES

NOTES

#51612—180 Days of Problem Solving